In *Be Holy: Learning the Path of Sanctification*, my friend Jason Garwood gives us a crisp and clear treatment of biblical holiness that will rock the illusion of self-righteousness. With biblical precision, he gives us simple, yet profound insights. *Be Holy* will serve as an indispensable teaching tool for many years to come. You may just have to rethink the way you view holiness altogether. Read it, teach it, preach it . . . often!

—**Pastor Doug Logan, Jr.**, Lead Pastor & Founder of Epiphany Fellowship of Camden NJ.

Holiness is a challenging concept that Jason Garwood has done a great job in breaking down to help us understand it. Let's not let the challenge of sanctification keep us from engaging in a lifelong pursuit of holy living."

—**Phil Whipple,** Bishop of the Church of the United Brethren in Christ, USA.

*Be Holy* is a timely and modern primer on the doctrine of sanctification. The book takes a clear and direct approach to the issue at hand, expressing deep truths in a concise manner. Jason issues a straightforward and provoking "call to arms" for all followers of Jesus.

—**Marc Herron**, Associate Pastor of First Baptist Church, Caro, MI

We are living in a time (and culture) when great confusion exists in the Church regarding how we are to grow in Christ. While many people rightly teach the biblical balance between grace and effort in the Christian life—some overemphasize grace to the neglect of effort . . . . This is why I'm thrilled to recommend *Be Holy: Learning the Path of Sanctification*. Garwood understands firsthand the struggles people face because he deals with them every day in his own life and pastoral ministry. He writes to help Christians and the Church to think through the issue at hand in order to more fully understand what sanctification means. . . . Jason follows in the tradition of the Reformers and the Puritans, and contemporary authors like John Piper and Kevin DeYoung, who understand this biblical balance. I highly recommend *Be Holy* and pray the Lord will powerfully use it in the life of His people, and for the edification of the Church, for His glory.

—**Dave Jenkins,** Executive Director of Servants of Grace Ministries and Executive Editor, Theology for Life Magazine

"Pursuing holiness will often hurt but it also helps and heals. In his book *Be Holy,* Jason Garwood carefully curates a thesis that practically explains why being holy may not be popular but it must be pursued. Taking the fabric of the full gospel, the book connects the theological with the practical. After reading this book, the reader will be inspired to not just hope to live a holy life but rather will be able to experience it—not because of what they do, but because of what Jesus has already done."

—**Bogdan Kipko,** Author Of *Forward: How To Get Unstuck & Become Unstoppable.*

In *Be Holy,* Jason Garwood tackles sanctification, a subject that is often talked about but rarely considered in its entirety, in a fresh and accessible way. A talented writer and able theologian, Garwood makes the doctrine of sanctification relevant without sacrificing robust, biblical depth. Read this and be encouraged in your faith!

—**Brandon D. Smith,** Editor of *Make, Mature, Multiply: Becoming Fully-Formed Disciples of Jesus* and Associate Editor of the Criswell Theological Review.

LEARNING THE PATH OF SANCTIFICATION

BY

JASON M. GARWOOD

FOREWORD BY MATHEW B. SIMS

# BE HOLY

## Learning the Path of Sanctification

JASON M. GARWOOD

GRACE FOR SINNERS BOOKS

Copyright ©2014 by Jason M. Garwood
*All rights reserved. No part of this publication may be reproduced in any form without written permission from the author. Made and designed in the United States of America.*

ISBN-13: 978-0692350287
ISBN-10: 0692350284

Scripture quotations are from The Holy Bible, English Standard Version® (ESV®), copyright © 2001 by Crossway, a publishing ministry of Good News Publishers. Used by permission. All rights reserved.

Cover design by Brett A. Garwood, redbagmedia.com

**TO THE CHURCH CALLED COLWOOD:**

Let us pursue the Holy One with unwavering fervor

# TABLE OF CONTENTS

Acknowledgements 11
Foreword **by Mathew. B Sims** 13

Introduction 17
Chapter One **The Demand** 19
Chapter Two **The Misery of the Heart** 31
Chapter Three **It's Not Legalism** 45
Chapter Four **Make War** 59
Chapter Five **Holiness and the Church** 71
Chapter Six **Holiness and Joy** 85

About the Author
More Resources from G4S Books

# ACKNOWLEDGEMENTS

I first want to thank my wife Mary for loving me unconditionally. Thank you for always supporting me in my writing. You are a helpmeet beyond imagination. To my children, Elijah, Avery and Nathan: you are an incredible blessing to me. May the Spirit provoke your little hearts every day. I love you all so very much!

A *major* thanks to Mathew B. Sims for reading this manuscript, offering up some wonderful insight, and making it better. Your editing is superb. Thank you for helping me write gooder.

Many thanks to the men and women I have the joy and privilege of serving alongside at Colwood Church. My staff, our Elders and Deacons: thank you for loving Jesus more than me.

Thank you Jesus for your obedience on my behalf. Without your righteousness I stand no chance before the Throne.

Soli Deo Gloria

# FOREWORD

Over the last four years plus, the church has renewed an age old intramural conversation on the doctrine of sanctification. Here are some of the questions I'm hearing:

- *Is it only by fixing our eyes on the cross of Christ one is sanctified?*
- *Does our effort play any part in our sanctification?*
- *Do we move past the gospel in sanctification?*
- *Are justification and sanctification accomplished differently?*

The solution isn't either/or. It's *Yes and Amen.* Let me explain. One central truth draws these sides close together. Prior to conversion we are alienated from God. We can do *good* (the *common grace* kind), but we cannot do *righteousness* before God (the *saving grace* kind), not the kind that pleases a holy God. We need *Someone* to step in and fundamentally transform our constitution. We were dead unto righteousness. We were dead unto God. Jesus steps in baptizing us from death unto life. From then on out we are inseparably united *together* in Christ.

Once we are in Christ everything changes. God looks upon us and says, "This is my beloved Son, with whom I am well pleased" (Matt. 3:17). We change positionally, forensically. We were enemies of God, but the covenant of peace has been sealed with the blood of Christ through justification by faith. In the eyes of the Highest Court's Judge, we are not guilty and righteous in Christ.

*In Christ,* we can please God. God delights in our obedience because he sees Christ when he sees us. God delights in our striving after him because he sees Christ when he sees us. God delights in our meager efforts in living a life of faith because he sees Christ when he sees us. That doesn't negate what Luther describes as living a life of repentance. Our cry is always and often, "Lord, I repent for my daily sin."

So are we sanctified by fixing our gaze on the cross of Christ? *Yes!* We live beneath the cross.

Does our effort play any part in our sanctification? Yes in Christ we live, breathe, and love by the power of the Holy Spirit. We strive, work, and believe *in Christ*. Synergism is the wrong word here. There's not two parties working alongside of each other. There's one *united body in Christ working in the power of the Spirit.*

Do we move past the gospel in sanctification? Absolutely not. The gospel raised us from death to life and unites us with Christ forever. We no more move past the gospel than a child moves beyond breathing as they mature.

Are justification and sanctification accomplished differently? They are accomplished by the work of God through the person of Jesus in the power of the Spirit. Both are intrinsically trinitarian. We do not subtract in sanctification. We are *added into Christ and act in the Spirit*. Jesus is our Head and we are his Body. Sanctification draws us into communion and union with God.

You see? It's not either/or. We strive after holiness. We act in love for God and neighbor as the Body of our beloved Head. You could no more separate what my head does from what my body does than you could separate me from Christ. Jesus Christ is our *Yes and Amen* as we strive, make every effort, and obey God. All of this is *in Christ*. We are *fully* sanctified *in Him*.

Paul sums up perfectly the life we now live in Christ,

> But if, in our endeavor to be justified in Christ, we too were found to be sinners, is Christ then a servant of sin? Certainly not! For if I rebuild what I tore down, I prove myself to be a transgressor. For through the law I died to the law, so that I might live to God. *I have been crucified with Christ. It is no longer I who live, but Christ who lives in me. And the life I now live in the flesh I live by faith in the Son of God, who loved me and gave himself for me.* I do not nullify the grace

> of God, for if righteousness were through the law, then Christ died for no purpose. (Gal. 2:17-21 italics mine)

Jason Garwood understands the importance of sanctification. It isn't a dollar store doctrine. We miss its import to our own peril. I recently came across this quotation, "'Wrongdoing' implies no particular narrative, whereas 'sin' comes from a religious tradition that insists on the possibility of redemption."[1] The author of Hebrews discussing our battle with sin and suffering in this world says, "Strive for peace with everyone, and for the holiness without which no one will see the Lord" (12:14). When we see our sin in light of a holy God, we also see that only Jesus Christ can meet that need. We see that there's hope for redemption, sanctification now, and glorification ultimately. We are blessed by God "in Christ with every spiritual blessing in the heavenly places" (Eph. 1:3). Jason shines a light on the Trinitarian work of God in the gospel—for our sanctification. Rest in Him. Strive after the holiness with which you cannot see Him without.

**Mathew B. Sims**
Managing Editor, Gospel-Centered Discipleship
Assistant Editor, CBMW Men's Channel

---

[1] www.Twitter.com/PrestonSprinkle 11/18/14
https://twitter.com/PrestonSprinkle/status/534914774790713344

# INTRODUCTION

*I'm so confused. You tell me that I can grow in my Christian walk but I don't see how that's possible. You don't know what I've done and I don't know what to do. I turned from my sin and received Jesus, but now what? What's next?*

If you're anything like me, you've wrestled with these questions about sanctification. You've wrestled with what true growth looks like in your life. Maybe you came to faith at a young age and thought that sanctification was something you could "get to," but you never actually got there, so to this day you're filled with disillusionment. Maybe your expectations of holiness were rooted in legalism. Either way, there's something missing and you don't know what it is.

Truth be told, there has been a deep-seated discomfort in my soul for a long time. The problem? *Sanctification.* The problem with sanctification? *Me.* The problem with me? A wrong view of the holiness of God and the law and the gospel, an obscure understanding of my heart and how it functions, a conflated understanding of justification and sanctification, a wrong view of the Holy Spirit and His role in my day-to-day life, an unclear understanding of the church, a defeatist eschatology, and a belief that somehow Christians should never be happy. (It took me a long time to realize all of this, as you might well imagine.)

My aim is to help you think through some different categories as it pertains to the path of sanctification that we would do well to heed. The tension I want you to avoid is thinking that you are about to get a "self-help" book with "five-full-proof-steps to a better plan for success and prosperity in God's irrefutable promises of leaving a legacy." Without hesitation, there will be things for us to consider as it pertains to the head, heart and hands. These things will require massive inventory of your faculties. But this is not a "quick-fix"; it's a "soul examination" sort of thing.

*Be Holy* is an introduction to the doctrine of sanctification and holiness. Prayerfully make your way through it. Look up the various Scriptures—don't just see . . . taste as well. To encourage further growth in holiness, I have referred throughout to various works for you to consider.

That said, I promised some people to keep this short, so let's get right to work.

CHAPTER ONE

# THE DEMAND

"Be Holy, for I am Holy."

Holiness is not a cute suggestion. It's not a pragmatic recommendation, either. It's not a footnote in the grand-narrative of Scripture, nor is it one option among many. It is an executive order from the highest office in the universe. Indeed, we are commanded—dare I say, demanded?—to be holy because God is holy. To be holy is to be set apart, consecrated to God for His purposes. Holiness is connected to the word "sanctify," which denotes a cleansing from sin and moral defilement. Think of holiness in terms of moral purity, which is the goal of our redemption.[2] If we are to understand the path of sanctification, we must first understand the holiness of God.

## THE HOLINESS OF GOD

In Isaiah 6, the prophet is given a glimpse of the pre-incarnate Son of God, Jesus (Jn. 12:41), the second person of the Trinity,

> In the year that King Uzziah died I saw the Lord sitting upon a throne, high and lifted up; and the train of his robe filled the temple. Above him stood the seraphim. Each had six wings: with two he covered his face, and with two he covered his feet, and with two he flew. And One called to another and said: "Holy, holy, holy is the LORD of hosts; the

---

[2] J.I. Packer, *Rediscovering Holiness: Knowing the Fullness of Life with God* (Ventura, CA: Regal, 2009), 33.

> whole earth is full of his glory!" And the foundations of the thresholds shook at the voice of him who called, and the house was filled with smoke. —Isaiah 6:1-4

What an amazing sight this must have been! Isaiah sees the Lord of glory in the fullness of His splendor, and because the picture is so beautiful, words can barely describe it.

Isaiah notices a few things in his vision. To start, he sees the "Lord," meaning, *adonai,* the "sovereign one."[3] This is the title given to YHWH. Isaiah sees the one true God in all of His glory. Notice that he also sees the train of the Lord's robe. In royal contexts, the train of a king or queen is symbolic of splendor, authority, and supremacy. Isaiah says that the Lord's train filled the entire temple. Why? Because He is King—the King of kings, to be sure—and His robe trumps all other robes.

Isaiah also sees the seraphim with wings worshiping God in all His transcendent majesty as they sing, "Holy, holy, holy." He is the thrice holy God. He is never described as, "Loving, loving, loving," or "Gracious, gracious, gracious." God is not described as anything else in Scripture using a word three times, except for when described by His holiness. The worship of God for all eternity is founded upon the holiness of God. He is *infinitely* holy.

When the Bible describes God and His attributes, holiness takes precedence. To be holy is to be set apart; holiness is God's "set-apartness." He's different. Moreover, He's *transcendent*, meaning that He is "out there" and completely distinct and different from His creation, and *majestic*, meaning that His moral qualities are perfect and without sin. For something or someone to be "holy" is for that object or person to be free from the toxicity of sin. God is morally pure and morally perfect. As Jerry Bridges put it, God "cannot but *know* what is right"; therefore, "He cannot but *do* what is right."[4]

---

[3] R.C. Sproul, *The Holiness of God* (Carol Stream, IL: Tyndale, 1998), 18.

[4] Jerry Bridges, *The Pursuit of Holiness* (Colorado Springs, CO: NavPress, 2006), 22. Emphasis in the original.

Because God is holy, He cannot help but do that which coincides with His character. Yes, He is perfect and only does what is right, but He also never wavers from His perfect self. God cannot help but be God all the time. Malachi proclaims, "For I the LORD do not change" (3:6). He is never wrong, never unsure, and never sinful. God is supremely perfect in all of His character and attributes, and His holiness permeates everything about Him. This is our God!

So what is our response as covenant law-breakers (sinners) who fail to live up to this perfect standard of righteousness? If God demands holiness from His creatures, and they cannot attain it themselves due to their nefarious natures, what happens? We will explore this through the rest of the book. Let us first look at the sinfulness of man.

## THE SINFULNESS OF MAN

Take note of what Isaiah does following this brief glimpse into the throne room of God:

> And I said: "Woe is me! For I am lost; for I am a man of unclean lips, and I dwell in the midst of a people of unclean lips; for my eyes have seen the King, the LORD of hosts!" — Isaiah 6:5

The only appropriate response to the holiness of God is a serious reassessment of yourself. When we see God for who He really is, we then in turn see ourselves for who we really are. Isaiah pronounces a curse on himself having seen the glory of God! He describes himself as being lost, needing mediation because of his impurity. The transcendent majesty of God stuns the prophet by making him reexamine himself. Not only this, Isaiah knows that his fellow countrymen are unclean as well! They as a nation have broken the covenant.

If we were to describe sin as the Bible does, it would take an entire book. From moral impurity, to the transgression of God's law, and missing the mark, the Bible describes sin in various ways with various nuances and angles. For our purposes here in this chapter, I simply want to point out that Isaiah's sin is revealed in the *pure perfection and light* of God. Sin is doing anything that violates God's law, but it is also not doing something in light of revealed truth. For Isaiah, as well as us, sin is the maligning of God's holy perfection.

Consequently, we can label sin for what it truly is: evil. It is anti-God. It is the transgression of the covenant and the stipulations found in God's law. It is, to put it in the Apostle Paul's terms, a falling "short of the glory of God" (Rom. 3:23). If we are to see ourselves for who we really are, we must compare ourselves with God, and not others. When the perfect rule of God is held up in front of us, we simply fall short every single time. Sin is a horrible curse because it is against a magnificent God. You and I are deeply flawed and until we get to the place where we are willing to admit it, we will continue to entertain ourselves with denial until we are dead.

Oftentimes when we think about holiness we think about ourselves and our personal pietistic endeavors. We need to start, however, with the holiness of God. Make no mistake, you are probably better than the person next to you. That's always the case because when we compare ourselves horizontally, we set up our own law and it just so happens that we meet the criterion every single time, but "they" do not. But we should not be concerned with living to impress others. No, our job is to be conformed to God and His character. That is the demand. If sin is the destruction of God's image in us, then sanctification is the restoration of Christ's image in us. We start with the holiness of God, and because of that, we see our sin for what it truly is. Heinous. Deplorable. Disgraceful. Reprehensible. Lamentable. Appalling. Inexcusable.

## YOUR VIEW OF GOD MATTERS

I grew up with the understanding that God was like Santa Claus—make sure you're on the 'good list' because the 'naughty list' will not be pleasant for you. I don't believe I was intentionally taught to think like this, it just sort of happened. If I do good things and avoid bad things, well, then I guess I'm going to be OK. Unfortunately the journey for me to understand the nature of God and His glorious gospel was a long, arduous process.

When we talk about the path of sanctification, we have to be clear what our view of God is like. For many of us, our view of God isn't much different than the god of other monotheistic religions (and maybe polytheistic ones, too!). Sometimes we see God the Father as an angry drunk uncle waiting to unleash His fury if we bother Him one more time. Others see God as impotent and unable to meet our needs when we need it. *Your view of God directly affects your path towards holiness.* Christian, let me help for a moment.

A friend of mine made a statement to me just a few short weeks ago that was startling at best. He was describing his view of God as a kid, "The God I grew up with was not the God of the Bible." In context, he was sharing his experience in a fundamentalist church that viewed God as a stern, angry father who was waiting to drop the hammer if you made one wrong move. Instead of believing that the Father looks on us and sees His Son in our place, he was taught that God was angry with him pretty much all the time. Instead of freedom in the good news of Christ in our place, he suffered from the bondage of bad news that said he couldn't make God happy enough. Instead of seeing himself as a son of God, he saw himself as an orphan without a family. Once he began to understand the gospel, things changed for him.

Your view of God absolutely matters when we talk about the path towards sanctification!

Now, unless we forget something important: God absolutely hates sin In Habbukuk 1:13, the prophet says, "You who are pure eyes than to see evil, and cannot look at wrong." He hates sin because it is completely antithetical to Himself. To be sure, God is a judge who will bring all men into judgment (Ecc. 12:14), even the secrets of men (Rom. 2:16). God's wrath against sin is in response to the violation of His holiness, and in His perfect judgment. Sinners will either pay the fine themselves in hell, or sinners will repent and trust that Christ's atonement will suffice to foot the bill. Either way, God proves himself to be just, and the justifier (Rom. 3:26). At the cross we see both God's hatred towards sin and His love for sinners. Living the gospel-centered life starts with these realities: when we contemplate God's holiness, we realize how much He hates sin, but we do not fall into despair because at the cross we also see His love for us, and that is encouraging. We *can* obey Him (Deut. 30:11) because He *is* good (Ps. 73:1). How you view God is directly related to how you grow as a believer. When we pour over the Scriptures, searching to learn about God, the path of holiness is illuminated (Ps. 119:105).

## THE SERIOUSNESS OF SANCTIFICATION

In case you have yet to feel the weight of this discussion on holiness, the author of Hebrews says, "Strive for peace with everyone, and for the holiness without which no one will see the Lord" (12:14).

If you will not be holy, then you will not see the Lord. Now, let me give some context before we swing the pendulum too far. Hebrews 12:14 does not make sense unless you read it with Hebrews 10:10, which says, "And by that will [the unchanging purposes of God] we have been sanctified through the offering of the body of Jesus Christ once for all." I would also mention that Paul says in 1 Corinthians 1:30 that Christ became our sanctification.

Sanctification is serious business. If we are to be holy as God is holy, then we must take sin seriously just as God takes sin seriously. It is here where we must define some technical jargon. There are two basic concepts related to holiness and sanctification (and I use these terms interchangeably throughout this book). The first is *positional*, or, *definitive* holiness, and the second is the *process* of holiness, often called *progressive* sanctification.[5]

Positional/definitive holiness describes what Hebrews 10:10 says about us and what Christ has done on our behalf. Because we are *in Him*, we are given a status of holy. We are justified (legally declared to be righteous), redeemed (bought out of slavery to sin), adopted (we are now His children), and sanctified

---

[5] See Kevin DeYoung, *The Hole in Our Holiness: Filling the Gap Between Gospel Passion and the Pursuit of Godliness* (Wheaton, IL: Crossway, 2012), 33ff.

(set apart for Him) all because of the gospel. This is our position before God. This is what Paul means in 1 Corinthians 1:2,

> To the church of God that is in Corinth, to those *sanctified in Christ Jesus*, called to be saints together with all those who in every place call upon the name of our Lord Jesus Christ, both their Lord and ours.

Because of the legal nature of justification, our sanctification is secure. This is also what Paul is getting at in Philippians 1:6, "And I am sure of this, that he who began a good work in you *will bring it to completion* at the day of Jesus Christ." Paul makes plain that positional holiness as a work of God inside of the believer,

> Therefore, my beloved, as you have always obeyed, so now, not only in my absence, work out your own salvation with fear and trembling, for *it is God who works in you*, both to will and to work for his good pleasure. —Philippians 2:12-13

The doctrine of positional holiness is the consistent teaching of Scripture. Christ has made us holy because He is the Holy One of God.[6] What Hebrews 12:14 describes is the ongoing process of sanctification *that is our responsibility to do*. The first fuels the second. When we accurately understand our positional holiness, the process of holiness goes a lot smoother. Maybe thinking about it in terms of past, present, and future will help. We *were* made holy through Christ's substitutionary death and resurrection, and subsequent justification by faith alone; we *are being made* holy through the Spirit's application of the work of Christ in our life; and we *will be completely holy* in the presence of our Holy Father in glory at the final resurrection.

---

[6] See, for example, Mark 1:24, Luke 4:34, John 6:69, and Revelation 3:7. Jesus is often called the "Holy One." It is also curious that He is sometimes called this by demons.

Jerry Bridges calls this dynamic, "Dependent responsibility." [7] It's the biblical truth that we are utterly and completely dependent on God for this process of sanctification, and yet in the same token, we are completely responsible for our own growth. Philippians 2:12-13 clearly teaches both.

The seriousness of sanctification cannot be overstated. In fact, one of the signs that you do not care about holiness is that you do not care about the seriousness of your sin. The demand is that we be holy, but we cannot do this by ourselves. However, because of Christ's work on the cross, the penalty of sin was paid, and thus we were made holy as we are in Him. This is huge! *Christ has met this demand for us, so that we can now go and freely obey Him out of love and gratitude.* Put differently, Christ saves a man and consecrates him all in the same salvific process: grace alone through faith alone, in Christ alone.

John Owen agrees,

> God has promised to sanctify us, to work this holiness in us; he does not leave us to do it by our own ability and power.[8]

## THE REASON WHY WE DO NOT CARE ABOUT HOLINESS

In *The Hole in Our Holiness*, Kevin DeYoung says that the major "hole" in our holiness is that, "a concern for holiness is not obvious in our lives like it's obvious in the pages of Scripture."[9] DeYoung's point is that we just don't care. I think he's right. Many today do not give a whole lot of thought to this demand to be holy, and because of it, we have unregenerate people playing "church." While I do not wish to paint such a broad stroke, the reality is, the statistics are there to back it up: the church in

---

[7] For a thorough treatment, see: Jerry Bridges, *The Transforming Power of the Gospel* (Colorado Springs, CO: NavPress, 2012), 105-117.

[8] John Owen, *The Holy Spirit*, abridged and simplified by R.J.K. Law (Edinburgh: Banner of Truth, 2012), 103.

[9] KevinDeYoung, *The Hole in Our Holiness: Filling the Gap Between Gospel Passion and the Pursuit of Godliness* (Wheaton, IL: Crossway, 2012), 17.[9]

America is suffering from theological anemia.[10] Because of it, holiness becomes a thing of the past.

There are many reasons why Christians do not care about sanctification. The first reason is that we do not understand the gospel. People who do not have clarity on the good news do not have clarity on holiness. The gospel is the proclamation that Christ has become King. It is the story of Israel brought to completion in the True Israelite, Jesus. It's about His virgin birth, born into the world free from sin; His perfectly obedient life under the law of God; His fulfillment of the aspirations of Israel as the Suffering Servant; His substitutionary death, justifying verdict in His resurrection from the dead, ascension to the throne, current mediation for His people, guarantee of salvation, and His promise to return—all of this is the gospel! It's news about the arrival of hope, and the triumph over evil. It's all about Jesus. If this is not understood, revisited, clarified, contemplated, applied, and rooted in the heart, holiness will not work, nor will there be sufficient motivation to want to do it.

The second reason that Christians do not care about holiness is that we have been told to "live the gospel." Listen, you and I are terrible saviors. You and I cannot be good news to people. No one "lives the gospel." This is a man-centered approach to holiness. The gospel depends on an empty cross and empty tomb, not you. "Living out the gospel" only happened once. Can you live out the implications of the gospel? Absolutely. Can you live *in light* of the gospel? Most assuredly. But you are not good news to people. Jesus is. Ultimately, this type of thinking is a denial of the true gospel of Jesus Christ.

Our third reason for not caring about holiness is the lack of clarity on the topic of repentance. I will spend more time on this in the next chapter, but suffice it to say at this point, that a lack of understanding about the nature of true biblical repentance will cripple any effort towards gospel-centered sanctification.

---

[10] Ligonier Ministries recently commissioned LifeWay to research the health of the church. The findings demonstrate the critical doctrinal anemia of the church. ligonier-static-media.s3.amazonaws.com/uploads/thestateoftheology/TheStateOfTheology-Infographic.pdf

Growing in repentance knows no limits. We grow most in godly repentance when we realize that we can always make much of God's grace in our lives. Instead of thinking of it as a "one-time" thing, we must persist in our beholding of God *daily*, confident that there is always opportunity for more repentance. Remember: God's kindness leads us to repentance (Rom. 2:4), and He has been exceedingly gracious. Sanctification becomes a problem when we minimize sin in our lives. True repentance does not minimize sin, it slays it. As God's holiness increases in our lives, so does ours.

One simply cannot catch a glimpse of the holiness of God and remain unmoved! He's majestic, beautiful, and pure; He's sovereign, perfect, and glorious! If you fail to see God and His infinite beauty, stare at Him until you see it (2 Cor. 3:18).[11]

## GOSPEL-CENTERED SANCTIFICATION

Back to Isaiah's encounter with God for a moment. The fuel for gospel-centered sanctification is found in Isaiah 6:7. Right before Isaiah is sent on a mission to prosecute Israel for her covenant disobedience, one of the seraphim touches Isaiah's mouth with a burning coal and says to Isaiah, "Behold, this has touched your lips; your guilt is taken away, and your sin atoned for." This moment, of course, foreshadows the atonement Christ made on the cross as a propitiatory sacrifice to end all previous sacrifices. The way guilt, shame, sin and transgression is done away with is through an atonement. This purification makes Isaiah a worthy minister of God, suitable to go and proclaim the excellencies of God.

Gospel-centered sanctification means that God the Holy Spirit who indwells us points our affections to the cross where we see both the holiness of God and the sinfulness that is within our hearts. The more we see the holiness of God, the more we love Him and see our sins for what they truly are. When we see the sinfulness of ourselves, we are reminded of the gospel—that

[11] For more on beholding and becoming, see "The Beauty of the Gospel in Discipleship." GCDiscipleship.com.
http://gcdiscipleship.com/the-beauty-of-the-gospel-in-discipleship/

God, in His holy love has rescued us, so that pride no longer rules us, and neither does despair. Gospel-centered sanctification is a constant ebb and flow between His holiness and my sin—the one always pointing to the other. When this happens, we desire to be holy because our hearts are gripped by good news. When we understand that the demand has been met in Christ in His work on the cross on our behalf (Gal. 3:13), the motivation towards holiness is clear. Once that is understood, the Spirit then uses that to spur us on towards holiness. The gospel is always at the center, both as the motivation, and the fuel. Now, if we could only understand the heart.

CHAPTER TWO

# THE MISERY OF THE HEART

Chapter thirteen, section one of the *Westminster Confession of Faith* defines sanctification this way:

> They, who are once effectually called, and regenerated, having a new heart, and a new spirit created in them, are further sanctified, really and personally, through the virtue of Christ's death and resurrection, by His Word and Spirit dwelling in them, the dominion of the whole body of sin is destroyed, and the several lusts thereof are more and more weakened and mortified; and they more and more quickened and strengthened in all saving graces, to the practice of true holiness, without which no man shall see the Lord.[12]

Notice that the conditions that makes sanctification possible involves not only an effectual call, but a regenerated or "new heart." Dead hearts cannot be holy unless resurrected by the work of the Spirit (Jn. 3:1-15). Consequently, efforts in sanctification will prove futile unless the heart is appropriately assessed. A heart that is made alive by sovereign grace is a heart suitable for sanctification. If we do not understand our heart, the pursuit of holiness will be driven by something other than

---

[12] *The Westminster Confession of Faith*. Oak Harbor, WA: Logos Research Systems, Inc., 1996. Print.

the gospel.

When discussing the centrality of the heart, Proverbs 4:23 is helpful. "Keep your heart with all vigilance, for from it flow the springs of life."

The heart is the central operating system for the soul. The heart is what drives the will (what we choose), the emotions (what we feel), and the mind (what we think). They all work together, of course, but the heart takes central stage in the drama of life. In the context of this verse, wisdom must be rooted in the heart so that the rest of our being can be suited for God's work, faithfully obeying God's law. Dallas Willard comments, "Put everything you have into the care of your heart, for it determines what your life amounts to."[13] The point is well made: your heart is what steers your life. Watch it, keep it, examine it, understand it, and protect it from sin.

> The heart of man plans his way, but the LORD establishes his steps. —Proverbs 16:9

> As in water face reflects face, so the heart of man reflects the man. —Proverbs 27:19

The importance of the heart is spelled out by God in Ezekiel 36:26, an anticipatory New Covenant promise:

> And I will give you a new heart, and a new spirit I will put within you. And I will remove the heart of stone from your flesh and give you a heart of flesh.

Because God sees the heart as the main problem, He sees a heart replacement as the main solution. But before we get too far ahead of ourselves, we need to dig further into the problem.

---

[13] *The Westminster Collection of Christian Quotations*, ed. Martin H. Manser (Louisville, KY: Westminster John Knox, 2001), 164.

## THE WICKEDNESS OF THE HEART

Jesus understood very well that man's plight was a direct result from the heart's disobedience to God's law. Read these words from Mark 7:14-23,

> And he called the people to him again and said to them, "Hear me, all of you, and understand: There is nothing outside a person that by going into him can defile him, but the things that come out of a person are what defile him." And when he had entered the house and left the people, his disciples asked him about the parable. And he said to them, "Then are you also without understanding? Do you not see that whatever goes into a person from outside cannot defile him, since it enters not his heart but his stomach, and is expelled?" (Thus he declared all foods clean.) And he said, "What comes out of a person is what defiles him. For from within, out of the heart of man, come evil thoughts, sexual immorality, theft, murder, adultery, coveting, wickedness, deceit, sensuality, envy, slander, pride, foolishness. All these evil things come from within, and they defile a person."

Because of Adam's failure to obey (Gen. 3:6-8), his guilt was imputed to all mankind (Rom. 5:12, 15-19), and now all fall short of God's glory (Rom. 3:23). We are born in iniquity (Ps. 51:5), bent towards sin, unable to do good (Rom. 3:10-18; Eccl. 7:20), and dead in our trespasses (Eph. 2:1). Man is totally depraved, unable to resurrect his dead heart without divine intervention (Job 14:4, 15:14; John 3:3-8), and completely helpless and powerless to change his condition (Prov. 20:9; Jer. 13:23).

Jesus says that what comes "out of the heart of man" is what defiles him. The stench of sin begins in the heart. Jeremiah 17:9-10 is clear,

> The heart is deceitful above all things, and desperately sick; who can understand it? "I the Lord search the heart and test the mind, to give every man according to his ways, according to the fruit of his deeds."

Proverbs 20:9 has much to say about this as well., "Who can say, 'I have made my heart pure; I am clean from my sin'?"

The heart cannot beat for the glory of God unless God makes it do so. For the believer in Christ declared to be holy and making efforts to be holy, he or she must constantly go back to the wickedness of the heart in order to make any progress. If the heart is not involved in the process of growth, you simply do not have growth. You will either fall into the sin of works righteousness, or the equally extreme sin of antinomianism.

## YOUR VIEW OF SIN MATTERS

Which is why your view of sin matters, too. If you think sin is simply a "mistake," "misjudgment," or "unfortunate event," then you will never do justice to your pursuit of holiness. John Owen gives us some insight:

> He is no true believer unto whom sin is not the greatest burden, sorrow, and trouble. Other things, as the loss of dear relations, or extraordinary pains, may make deeper impressions on the mind, by its natural affections, at some seasons than ever our sins did at any one time in any one instance,—so a man may have a greater trouble in sense of pain by a fit of the toothache, which will be gone in an hour, than in a hectic fever or consumption, which will assuredly take away his life,—but take in the whole course of our lives, and all the actings of our souls, in spiritual judgment as well as in natural affection, and I do not understand how a man can be a sincere believer unto whom sin is not the greatest burden and sorrow.[14]

What Owen makes plain is that true believers loathe their sin. There's a certain attitude that fills their hearts and minds when the Spirit convicts them. Christians do not enjoy sin, do not minimize sin, do not like self-justification, and could care less about entertaining the sin again. They see sin as burdensome

---

[14] John Owen, *The Works of John Owen*. Ed. William H. Goold. Vol. 7. (Edinburgh: T&T Clark), 333.

and heavy. The old English word *mortify* is their hearts cry because they do not dare offend their Savior again.

Mortification means putting sin to death. Not dwell on it, reason with it, or even try to resist it, but kill it. The Puritans made this a central focus and rightfully so. When our attitude towards sin becomes anything less than an all out war against it, we shrink God's holiness and increase our own self-righteousness. How you *view* sin affects how you *handle* sin in your life.

One of the more dangerous and prevailing notions in churches today is the McJesus version of Christianity. Because sin is not loathed, nor is worldliness hardly considered, Jesus becomes a fast-food product to be sold on the dollar menu. *Jesus-lite* is a Jesus who only wants you to feel good about yourself, never points out your sin because that would make you feel too uncomfortable, is always there when you need Him (which, let's be honest, is a rare occasion), and would much rather talk about sports than biblical doctrine.

If you were to ask me what doctrine the church in America needs most right now, I would say the Doctrine of God with *sola scriptura* not far behind it. Here's why: *idolatry*. The McJesus of what's left of Western Christendom is a god of idolatry. Just look at the bestselling books in your local Christian bookstore. Books about little boys going to heaven, therapeutic deism that is man-centered, books that offer you a best life right now experience so you don't have to feel the weight of sin, and the list goes on. There's nothing about repentance, nothing about holiness, and nothing about the real Jesus of Scripture. Many are worshiping a god in their own image and they will be damned for it.

> "It is easy indeed to see how, the victim of its own empty illusions, superstition mocks God whenever it tries to please him. It only fastens on the things which God expressly says means nothing to him. It ignores those which he has commanded and which he has said are acceptable to him; or else it openly rejects them. Therefore all who, wishing to honour God, set up religions of their own devising, are merely worshipping their own fantasies. For they would

> never have ventured to trifle with God if they had not first fashioned him according to their whims.[15]

It absolutely amazes me how so much of Christian living today is driven by emotions instead of truth. "You have to learn to follow your heart," one writer[16] exhorts. That is horrible, absolutely despicable advice. If circumstances dictate your life, then what happens when one day you get a job promotion? You love God more and think he's blessing you for that nice thing you did the other day. But what happens if your kid dies the next day from some freak accident? Suddenly your emotions are real and you question whether God really loves you or not. Will truth dictate your response?

How about this, instead of emotionalism and deistic therapy, do what God's law says. A correct understanding of God combats the aberrant understanding of sin. Truth wins. Always.

We've already established our view of God matters when it comes to sanctification, but your view of sin matters for sanctification. Sin is an awful thing to pleasure yourself with, and if it is not defeated by a gospel-centered, biblical understanding and definition of God, you will naturally minimize it and play it off as no big deal. When you start to do that, you have officially given up on holiness. But we must dig even deeper.

## THE WAR OF AFFECTIONS AND IDOLS

I borrowed the phrase that bears this chapter's name from Dr. Thomas Chalmers and his sermon-turned-booklet called, *The Expulsive Power of a New Affection.*[17] If you've never read this piece of gospel-centered literature, you're missing out; it's truly a gem worth reading several times over.

---

[15] John Calvin. *Institutes of the Christian Religion.* Banner of Truth (Edinburgh, 2014), 7

[16] Joel Osteen, *Your Best Life Now.* (New York: NY, Warner Faith, 2004), 96.

[17] Thomas Chalmers, *The Expulsive Power of a New Affection* (Minneapolis, MN: Curiosmith, 2014).

In this book, Chalmers makes the case for how idols are removed from our hearts. He argues that the heart cannot eject an idol from itself because it has no inherit capability to do this. Listen to his own words:

> The love of God and the love of the world are two affections, not merely in a state of rivalship, but in the state of enmity—and that so irreconcilable, that they cannot dwell together in the same bosom. We have already affirmed how impossible it were for the heart, by any in the elasticity of it's own, to cast the world away from it, and thus reduce itself to a wilderness. The heart is not so constituted; and the only way to dispossess it of an old affection, is by the expulsive power of a new one.[18]

In other words, the heart does not just get rid of an old affection. The heart easily clings to the things of this world, and in order to rid yourself of a sinful desire, a new affection must take its place.

Let me illustrate for a moment. My wife and I have three children. My youngest (age one) has proven to us that diaper changing time is his least favorite part of the day. Saying that he doesn't like it would be an understatement. I think sometimes he believes something bad is going to happen, like surgery or something, but he flails about on the changing table voicing his displeasure just about every single time. But I learned something important in this experience: if I give him a toy or something out of the ordinary for him to hold while he's getting a new diaper, he quiets down. Why? Because his heart was given a new focus—something to hold his attention for the next few moments so that his diaper can get changed. While the analogy breaks down if pressed too hard, I think the point has been made. When our hearts are given over to something more beautiful, namely Jesus, the old sinful idol (affection) is removed and replaced with something greater.

Chalmers again:

---

[18] Ibid., 19.

> In a word, if the way to disengage the heart from the positive love of one great and ascendant object is to fasten it in positive love to another, then it is not by exposing the worthlessness of the former, but thy addressing to the mental eye the worth and excellence of the latter, that all old things are to be done away, and all things are to become new.[19]

This doesn't mean that we treat sin as though it isn't sin. It also doesn't mean that we are careless towards it (indeed we must mortify it!). It means that it is *not enough to just denounce a sin*. Our affections must be stirred by something greater.

Perhaps another illustration will help. My youngest (the same little boy from the previous example) loves to climb stairs. He's not old enough to do it on his own, but that doesn't stop him. In our basement is a carpeted floor with carpeted stairs. For a child, this is a heavenly opportunity for fun. Oftentimes when I get home I take the kiddos downstairs and we play together. Sometimes we dance (I'm a terrible dancer), sometimes we wrestle, sometimes we watch the television, and other times we just throw bouncy balls around at each other giggling incessantly. Regardless of the situation and activity, however, my youngest always desires to climb the stairs by himself. He gets upset when told no, but persists in his endeavor. Here's my point: my son has endless options for pleasure that await him with the tons of toys given to him by his grandparents, yet he still insists on disobeying what he is told. I'm trying to protect him. But he won't have it.

The same is true for you, Christian. Endless pleasure awaits us (Ps. 16:11), yet we still insist on doing whatever our little hearts are content to want to do. Your desire, like my son's, is driving your will. It's not enough for my son to be told "No!" He must experience, enjoy, delight in, and take pleasure in the wonderful things that can come his way when he chooses obedience. This is Chalmers' point. Our hearts war inside of us, prowling around seeking a pleasure to devour. It's not enough

---

[19] Ibid., 18.

for the law to tell us “No!” We need a change of heart. If we do not persist in keeping watch over the heart, we will desire something else. It only takes a moment for that to change.

In Exodus 32, there is a familiar incident that helps us understand this concept even more. Moses was up on the mountain, and the Israelite people began wondering what was going on (vs. 1-2). Because of their boredom, they approach Aaron and ask that he help make them gods to follow after. God got them this far, they now needed someone else to get them to the Promise Land. So Aaron helps! He gathers the gold, makes a golden calf, and proclaims that this god brought them out of Egypt (vs. 2-4). (Even as I type this I’m blown away by this story yet again. The foolishness of it all!)

After this, Aaron built an altar (vs. 5) and the next day the people enjoyed a feast (vs. 6). At this point, God tells Moses to go back down the mountain to His people because “they have corrupted themselves” (vs. 7). The LORD further says, “they have turned aside quickly out of the way that I commanded them” (vs. 8). Now, stop for a moment. The LORD has just redeemed the Israelites, and though the journey was a bit rough, they saw God’s mighty hand miraculously rescue them from slavery. Their leader, Moses, is up on the mountain receiving the Suzerain’s instructions for His vassals, and they “quickly” fall into idolatry. What happened?

Their hearts happened. They had forgotten in a moment’s notice the power of God and turned their affections elsewhere. How foolish does that make someone look? Consider Aaron’s excuse, which, in my estimation, is the worst excuse in the history of mankind. When asked what happened, Aaron replied to his brother,

> Let not the anger of my lord burn hot. You know the people, that they are set on evil. For they said to me, ‘Make us gods who shall go before us. As for this Moses, the man who brought us up out of the land of Egypt, we do not know what has become of him.’ So I said to them, ‘Let any who have gold take it off.’ So they gave it to me, and I threw it into the fire, and out came this calf. —Exodus 32:22-24

I literally laugh out loud every time I read this. Aaron created this calf, yet he defends himself by saying that they just threw in the gold and out popped this idol. Idols are deceptive sometimes (but they don't just show up without an invitation!), and lest we get self-righteous, remember that you and I do the very same things. We make excuses for our idols instead of making all out war on them. Get distracted for just one minute, and you end up with a golden calf in your lap. Make. War.

Affections are those things that we desire and long for. For example, I love University of Michigan football. But there was a time when I used to get so frustrated when my team lost (a rare occasion). Then I realized that I had a problem. You see, it was much easier for me to cry over a football game than it was to cry over my own indwelling sin. A lot of this is perspective, sure, but a lot of it is attitude as well. Affections are easily manipulated towards sin, and oftentimes difficult to control towards Godliness. Desiring God above all other things which vie for your attention inherently means casting off those things that are not godly. For me that means sometimes turning off the game and taking a moment to pray or play with my kids. For you it may mean something different. But for both of us, it means that if we are going to get serious about relying on the good news of the gospel and doing some serious heart assessment, we must work inside the realm of repentance.

## THE GOSPEL OF REPENTANCE

Those who wish to be holy are those who mourn over indwelling sin, not minimizing it, self-medicating with false contrition or justifying it, but rather mortifying it, putting to death the sin the lurks behind the heart. At the center of this is the biblical doctrine of repentance.

*Westminster Confession of Faith* 15:2 describes repentance for us,

> By it, a sinner, out of the sight and sense not only of the danger, but also of the filthiness and odiousness of his sins, as contrary to the holy nature, and righteous law of God; and upon the apprehension of His mercy in Christ to such as are penitent, so grieves for, and hates his sins, as to turn

from them all unto God, purposing and endeavouring to walk with Him in all the ways of His commandments.

Repentance is a change of mind, direction, will, and emotion. Here is a biblical look at repentance:

> "Therefore I will judge you, O house of Israel, every one according to his ways, declares the Lord God. Repent and turn from all your transgressions, lest iniquity be your ruin. Cast away from you all the transgressions that you have committed, and make yourselves a new heart and a new spirit! Why will you die, O house of Israel? —Ezekiel 18:30-31
>
> Then you will remember your evil ways, and your deeds that were not good, and you will loathe yourselves for your iniquities and your abominations. —Ezekiel 36:21
>
> Then you will defile your carved idols overlaid with silver and your gold-plated metal images. You will scatter them as unclean things. You will say to them, "Be gone!" —Isaiah 30:22
>
> Against you, you only, have I sinned and done what is evil in your sight, so that you may be justified in your words and blameless in your judgment. —Psalms 51:4
>
> "Yet even now," declares the Lord, "return to me with all your heart, with fasting, with weeping, and with mourning; and rend your hearts and not your garments." Return to the Lord your God, for He is gracious and merciful, slow to anger, and abounding in steadfast love; and he relents over disaster. —Joel 2:12-13
>
> Therefore I consider all your precepts to be right; I hate every false way. —Psalms 119:128
>
> I acknowledged my sin to you, and I did not cover my iniquity; I said, "I will confess my transgressions to the Lord," and you forgave the iniquity of my sin. —Psalms 32:5

The very first word of the gospel of the kingdom is "repent" (Mk. 1:15). Repentance is a change of mind, change of attitude towards sin (you are sorry for it), acknowledgment that you did it, prayer for forgiveness of the *specific sin*, a belief in the gospel of Jesus that realigns where you went off track, an obedience to God's law, and a tireless search for more repentance in your life. It is ongoing. We are to "bear fruit in keeping with repentance" (Matt. 3:8) because God "commands all people everywhere to repent" (Acts 17:30).

In sanctification, what we lean on for meaning, purpose, and identity—both in happiness and in misery—is our functional motivation for growth. If it's anything other than the gospel, we have crossed the line into idolatry. This ties in to the differences between attrition and contrition. The former is sorrow because you got caught; the latter is Godly sorrow and penitence because you've offended God. The first is man-centered, the second is God-centered. If we do not rely on the gospel of Jesus Christ to focus our view of the law, specifically the law's role in the believer, then we will not adequately deal with sin. The good news of repentance is that through the work of the Spirit, you can get to the heart, because, "Holiness is nothing but the implanting, writing, and realizing of the gospel in our souls."[20]

Repentance is the realization that you can no longer trust yourself. In other words, you cannot trust your bought-with-a-price-made-new nature that still enjoys the sinful thought or two (even though you are no longer under the dominion of sin!) because the sinful flesh's natural response to sin is to downplay it. Sin denies itself. You can't trust your emotions, you can't always trust what the world thinks. Repentance trusts what God thinks. You see, sanctification is oftentimes aligning your heart and emotions with the truth of God's word. Jesus prayed to the Father in John 17:17 to, "Sanctify [us] in the truth; your word is

---

20 John Owen, *The Works of John Owen*. Ed. William H. Goold. Vol. 3. (Edinburgh: T&T Clark), 370-371.

truth." The Spirit sanctifies us when the Word of God takes primacy in our lives.

The worship of the Triune God involves our heads, hearts and hands, but if truth does not prevail, the danger of emotionalism and works righteousness comes into play. For example, if we simply go with our hearts, as explained previously, truth will not guide our thinking. If we do not work out our sanctification *from* our justification (declared to be righteous and holy), then we will work out our sanctification *to* our justification, which is the problem of works righteousness (more on this in the next chapter).

So what do we *do*?

We preach the gospel to ourselves. Tell your soul how great God is until your heart bends to that truth. Tell your soul to "hope in God" (Ps. 42:5). Tell your mind to think on heavenly things (Col. 3:2). Tell your hands to work in the Lord because it's not in vain (1 Cor. 15:58). This process is rediscovering the wonder, beauty, and awe of the gospel. Tim Keller is helpful. "The key to continual and deeper spiritual renewal and revival is the continual re-discovery of the gospel."[21]

Your soul needs to be realigned to the truth of God's word. Tim Chester has written a wonderful book on the subject of change and I highly recommend it. In *You Can Change*, he describes the "4G's" that can help with this realignment process. The four G's about God are:

- *God is great—so we do not have to be in control.*
- *God is glorious—so we do not have to fear others.*
- *God is good—so we do not have to look elsewhere.*
- *God is gracious—so we do not have to prove ourselves.*

These truths are meant to be a "powerful diagnostic too for address most of the sins and emotions with which we struggle."[22]

Whether it is an attitude, emotion, insecurity, or behavior, truths such as these serve as an avenue to proclaim the good

---

[21] Tim Keller, "The Centrality of the Gospel," available online, http://download.redeemer.com/pdf/learn/resources/CentralityoftheGospel-Keller.pdf.

[22] Tim Chester, *You Can Change* (Wheaton, IL: Crossway, 2010), 80.

news of the gospel to ourselves and to each other. Since God is great, we do not have to control people or situations. He is sovereign over all and His providence is for my good. Since God is glorious, I need not fear other people, nor be crippled by the thought of having to impress them, because I fear God more. God is good, which means He is the one true source of infinite satisfaction and unending pleasure, so I need not look anywhere else for it. Finally, God is gracious, and because of His unending mercies that are new each day, I have nothing to prove, or earn. I can rest in His justifying verdict over my life. It's not enough to just hate sin; we must replace those affections with bigger truths.

I often tell my congregation to look and stare at the cross throughout each day. What I mean is, "Look at the cross, see your need and how helpless you are, and in the same look, see how sufficient He is for you! Look again, and again, and again!" The gospel is *the* proclamation to end all false proclamations promised by sin, idols and evil. The heart is miserable apart from Christ. And so we repent with faith over and over again, refusing to deny our sin, lest we make God a liar (1 Jn. 1:8-10), and instead choosing obedience.

CHAPTER THREE

# IT'S NOT LEGALISM

Sometimes we forget that the New Covenant is just that: a covenant. Like other covenants in the ancient Near East, the New Covenant has 1) an authority figure (Jesus is Lord); 2) a chain of command (we are His vice regents sent on mission under His authority); 3) a law to follow; 4) sanctions to remember ("do this, and this happens"); and lastly, 5) an inheritance that awaits ("the meek shall inherit the earth"). In other words, the New(er) Covenant fulfills the Old(er) Covenant and is still very much alive, demanding our obedience. There are blessings for obedience, and consequences for disobedience. Which path will we choose?

Jesus has much to say regarding this obedience:

> Whoever believes in the Son has eternal life; whoever does not obey the Son shall not see life, but the wrath of God remains on him. —John 3:36
>
> If you love me, you will keep my commandments. —John 14:15
>
> Whoever has my commandments and keeps them, he it is who loves me. And he who loves me will be loved by my Father, and I will love him and manifest myself to him. —John 14:21
>
> If you keep my commandments, you will abide in my love, just as I have kept my Father's commandments and abide in

> his love. —John 15:10

My contention in this chapter is simple: *obeying God and His law is not legalism*. In fact, obedience, according to Jesus, is love. You *really* love God when you obey Him. Paul tells us in Romans 13:10 that, "Love is the fulfilling of the law." It's not legalism to obey what God commands. It is, however, legalism to think that obedience is meritorious in nature. In other words, since God is holy and demands that His creatures be holy like Him, we can respond to that by either embracing God as our Supreme Gift, trusting in the sufficiency of Christ's meritorious work on our behalf, or trust in ourselves thinking that somehow we can "work" our way to God by behaving well enough. One is obedience from a heart that has been bought by Christ, the other is from a heart that is far from Christ. Moreover, there is a difference between working *from* your justification and working *towards* your justification. This difference is what makes your sanctification work properly—the way God designed it to.

## INDICATIVES AND IMPERATIVES

The New Testament (as well as the Old) is replete with commands. We shouldn't be surprised at this. God is the holy One, we are the sinful ones, and He gets to call the shots. It makes sense for the Creator to tell the creation what to do. God is the conquering Suzerain (King) whose peace treaty (covenant law) with His vassals (the conquered people) contains requirements. For example, we are told to do justice and love kindness:

> He has told you, O man, what is good; and what does the Lord require of you but to do justice, and to love kindness, and to walk humbly with your God? —Micah 6:8

We are *told* to do this. We are also told to avoid foolish arguments (Titus 3:9); be glad (Matt. 5:12); be perfect (Matt. 5:48); be merciful like God (Lk. 6:36); be patient towards people (1 Thess. 514; 2 Tim. 2:24); be sober and pray (1 Pt. 4:7); be ready to give an answer for the hope that is within us (1 Pt. 3:15); be transformed (Rom. 12:2); be hospitable (Rom. 12:13); be followers (1

Cor. 11:1; Phil. 3:17; Eph. 5:1); be steadfast and unmoveable (1 Cor. 15:58); be of good comfort (2 Cor. 13:11); be of one mind (Rom. 12:16; 2 Cor. 13:11; Phil. 2:2; 1 Pt. 3:8); be tenderhearted towards one another (Eph. 4:32); be anxious for nothing (Phil. 4:6); be doers of the Word (Jas. 1:22); beware of false prophets (Matt. 7:15); and lastly, though I haven't exhausted every command, we are told to repent and believe the gospel (Mk. 1:15; Acts 17:30).

The Bible is full of these commands, and we call them imperatives. An imperative is a command in Scripture for us to act *because* of something that is true. Indicatives are those truths. Imperatives *presuppose* indicatives. The very nature of indicatives *cause* and *imply* that imperatives exist.

Let's look at 2 Peter 1:1-11 for a moment:

> Simeon Peter, a servant and apostle of Jesus Christ,To those who have obtained a faith of equal standing with ours by the righteousness of our God and Savior Jesus Christ: May grace and peace be multiplied to you in the knowledge of God and of Jesus our Lord.
>
> His divine power has granted to us all things that pertain to life and godliness, through the knowledge of Him who called us to his own glory and excellence, by which he has granted to us his precious and very great promises, so that through them you may become partakers of the divine nature, having escaped from the corruption that is in the world because of sinful desire.
>
> For this very reason, make every effort to supplement your faith with virtue, and virtue with knowledge, and knowledge with self-control, and self-control with steadfastness, and steadfastness with godliness, and godliness with brotherly affection, and brotherly affection with love. For if these qualities are yours and are increasing, they keep you from being ineffective or unfruitful in the knowledge of our Lord Jesus Christ. For whoever lacks these qualities is so nearsighted that he is blind, having forgotten that he was cleansed from his former sins. Therefore, brothers, be all the more diligent to confirm your calling and election, for if you practice these qualities you will never fall. For in this

> way there will be richly provided for you an entrance into the eternal kingdom of our Lord and Savior Jesus Christ.

Notice that in verse 5, Peter commands us to "make every effort," and then later in verse ten he says to "be all the more diligent to make your calling and election sure." Peter has just told us to *do* something. This is our responsibility. Remember, we are now working within the *progressive holiness* realm of sanctification. This is our part in the path of sanctification. But how can Peter say this? Shouldn't he be called a legalist for telling his believing community to do something when they are, in fact, free in Christ? Isn't that an abuse of grace? Here's how He can do this . . .

The indicatives (truths) of the gospel drive the imperatives of holiness. The gospel is an indicative with hundreds of imperatives that follow it. Because Jesus is King, *these things are expected.* We cannot ignore the first four verses and jump right to what we are commanded to do without proper context. Peter opens up his letter writing to "those who have obtained a faith of equal standing with ours by the righteousness of our God and Savior Jesus Christ" (v. 1). Though they are not apostles, they have a faith that is built on the rock-solid foundation of the righteousness of Christ imputed to them through faith—the same foundation Peter stands on (cf. Rom. 5:1). This is God's guarantee, as it were, that the justification received by faith is genuine and true.

But Peter doesn't stop here. He goes on to explain that God's power has given them everything they need for life and godliness (holiness), "through the knowledge of him who called us to his own glory and excellence" (vs. 3). Here, this knowledge of Christ is not an abstract concept, but a reality in salvation, because they are "partakers of the divine nature," having escaped the clutches of sin and its dominion (vs. 4). Their union with Christ takes center focus as an appropriate reality through which, ontologically and faithfully, they can pursue holiness.

"Because this is true," Peter says, "get to work." Because the gospel of Jesus has done *this,* you are to do *that.* The imperative given in verse 5 is built upon the indicatives of vs. 1-4. In order to pursue holiness in sanctification, we must make every effort with faith, virtue, knowledge, self-control, steadfastness, godliness, brotherly affection and love. The same Spirit who wrought in us the miracle of regeneration is the same Spirit who works grace in us when we make strides towards godliness. This is partly why Peter can say in verse 10 to "make your calling and election sure." The election of the Father is secure (2 Tim. 2:19), but oftentimes the assurance we feel is not. Those who wish to persevere in life are to "practice these qualities" because in doing so they will "never fall" (vs. 10) True conversion with God-given grace that diligently exercises faith is coupled with God's promise of salvation to those who believe (Matt. 10:22; John 6:37; Heb. 3:6). This is the formula for sanctification.

The indicatives fuel the imperatives. Truth drives action. The gospel gives power to obedience. Charles H. Spurgeon gives us warning about using our newfound freedom for sinful gain:

> Brethren, it is a precious doctrine that the saints are safe, but it is a damnable inference from it, that therefore they may live as they list. It is a glorious truth that God will keep his people, but it is an abominable falsehood that sin will do them no harm. Remember that God gives us liberty, not licence, and while he gives us protection he will not allow us presumption.[23]

So why do many shout, "Legalist!" at the thought of obedience?

## LEGALISM AND ANTINOMIANISM

In our Western culture, particularly in the United States, we are quite familiar with words like, "Freedom," "individualism," "grace," and "self-discovery." We love stories of victory and freedom, all in the name of self-progress. Rugged individualism marked by a false-promise of autonomous self-governance has invaded our souls, and the result is an obscure understanding

---

[23] Charles Haddon Spurgeon, *Exploring the Mind and Heart of the Prince of Preachers: Five-Thousand Illustrations Selected from the Works of Charles Haddon Spurgeon* (Oswego, IL: Fox River Press, 2005), 11.

of these words. When some hear the word, "Grace," they think *I can do whatever I want.* The Apostle Paul clearly shuts this down (Rom. 6:1-2). When some hear the word, "Freedom," they think *I'm allowed to act however I want no matter the consequences.* Again, Scripture shuts this down (1 Cor. 6:19-20). Though not many people use the phrase, "autonomy," the reality is, many see their own pursuit of happiness as being and doing whatever it is they see fit. The book of Ecclesiastes alone blows up the notion of human autonomy. Life under the sun is awful, and in the end, we just die (Eccl. 9:1-6). This is the logical consummation of a life without rules—a life built on our own standards.

There are many other reasons why Christians shudder at the thought of obeying God's law, but suffice it to say we have confused terms, dumbed down doctrine, and inserted self as the center of human existence. Whether we are skeptical of authority, or just plain selfish, we have a problem. While I do not have the time to get into the finer details of the role of the law in lives of all humans—both sinners and saints—I do want to point out that Jesus' attitude towards it was positive. Jesus understood that since God's holiness is unchanging, His standard is unchanging as well:

> Do not think that I have come to abolish the Law or the Prophets; I have not come to abolish them but to fulfill them. For truly, I say to you, until heaven and earth pass away, not an iota, not a dot, will pass from the Law until all is accomplished. Therefore whoever relaxes one of the least of these commandments and teaches others to do the same will be called least in the kingdom of heaven, but whoever does them and teaches them will be called great in the kingdom of heaven. —Matthew 5:17-19

There are two extremes that are capable of trapping us in this pursuit of holiness, and we would do well to define our terms and check them with Scripture. The first error is legalism; the second, antinomianism.

Legalism is a humanist approach to salvation and sanctification.

The formula for *legalism* is:

Jesus + My Good Works = Salvation.

The biblical formula for *salvation* is:

Jesus Alone + Grace Alone Through God-Given Faith Alone = Salvation.

The biblical formula for *sanctification* is:

Jesus + Christ's Righteousness + the Spirit's Work + Scripture/Prayer + My Feeble Attempts at Godliness + a Whole Lot of Repentance = Sanctification.

Legalism is the notion that anything I do *before* or *after* salvation has some sort of standing before God. This was the Galatian problem:

> Yet we know that a person is not justified by works of the law but through faith in Jesus Christ, in order to be justified by faith in Christ and not by works of the law, because by works of the law no one will be justified. —Galatians 2:16

The legal declaration in the courtroom of God, "Justified!" is only given to the sinner when he has repented and trusted Christ. The Judge nearly slammed down His gavel and said, "Condemned!" when Christ steps in and says, "He's mine." That is justification. Justification is a legal term that declares someone to be "in the right." Justification is the status someone has who trusts in Christ *alone* for salvation; and that status given says that it is just as though he or she had never sinned, and just as though he or she has always obeyed. It's a legal covenant signed with the Lamb's blood-stained pen. The atonement of Christ restores a covenant-breaker to the status of covenant-keeper.

You can't get that status by offering something up to God. Even our *righteousness* is polluted (Is. 64:6). Let's be clear: the only thing you and I bring to the table is our sin. That's it. The only "freedom" our will had before the Spirit's work of regeneration is the freedom to continue in rebellion against God's law. Salvation is for the meek, not the proud. Sinners who prop themselves up as self-righteously worthy candidates for salvation will not receive it. No one earns salvation by works except for the Son of God who earned it on your behalf. We do not keep the law *in order to be saved,* but we make efforts in keeping the law *because we are saved.* Salvation does not hinge upon my obedience, but instead Christ's obedience; however, my sanctification and obedience to God's law does hinge upon my appropriate understanding of salvation.

In terms of sanctification, the issue of legalism *can* still get in the way of godliness. Legalism works a little differently with regard to salvation, because it is impossible to earn it. But legalism in sanctification can become a problem because the *motivation* for godliness can be warped, meaning that often we still believe that our growth is something we earn. The legal verdict of justification is bestowed when belief in the gospel is executed. From there the believer *still* needs the gospel. No one grows in sanctification by moving on from the gospel. The gospel isn't the starting point, it *is the point*! True growth in the pursuit of holiness *continues to carry out that legal verdict in your life.* Our attitude towards good works is not meritorious, but humble service to Christ the King. To avoid legalism in your Christian growth absolutely requires an accurate view of justification. Believers are believers because *they still believe.* If we forget that new legal status we resort to legalism. A slave who is freed by his master does not move on in life by dwelling on his slavery, but on his newfound status.

This leads us to the other extreme: antinomianism. Antinomianism literally means, "Against the law." At the heart of this error is the thinking that God's law is utterly destroyed and no longer applicable because of the cross of Christ. Stated another way, the antinomian believes that their freedom in Christ trumps any obligation to God's law. They approach Romans 6:14 and say, "See, we are no longer under the law, but instead are under grace! Don't tell *me* what to do!" Failing to see the context, especially verses 12-13 where they are told *not* to let themselves go the way of sin, the antinomian errs when he mistakenly thinks that he doesn't need to obey the law. Paul's point in this passage is that the Christian is *done* violating God's law and can now joyfully go in obedience to it because he has been set free, not from the law, but from it's curse. Greg Bahnsen explains,

> Because we are no longer under the curse of the law and shut in to its inherent impotence in enabling obedience—because we are under *God's enabling grace,* not under law—we must not allow violations of the law [i.e., sin: 1 John 3:4] to dominate our lives. It is in order that the righteous ordinance of the law may be fulfilled in us that God has graciously put His Spirit within our hearts (Rom. 8:4).[24]

Because the curse has been fulfilled, and Christ became that curse for us, we are now free to obey as the Spirit works the gospel deep within our souls (Gal. 3:13). Sin's dominion over us was executed in the death of Christ (Rom. 6:14).

The mantra of the antinomian is, "Only God can judge me!" to which I respond, "That should be no comfort to you."

Again, grace enables us to obey. Christianity is not about bad people being made good, or even good people become better: it's about dead people being made alive. Dead hearts cannot obey God's law, but they can attempt to do so, thinking it will merit them favor. It is God who causes us to walk in His ways when He changes our hearts (Ez. 36:27).

The danger with these two errors is over-correcting. As I write this, we here in Michigan have had about two to three feet of snow on the ground since before Christmas (it's now February). Now, Michigan is known for people being able to drive in the snow, but the key to doing so is found in *not* over-correcting when you feel the car getting out of control. If you steer too far the other way, the car will whip around too fast and you'll end up in the ditch anyway. Sanctification is like driving in snowy Michigan. Don't over-correct. Don't feel like a legalist when you choose obedience over sin. Don't feel like an antinomian when the freedom you do have can be exercised in the name of Jesus (1 Cor. 10:31). We were created *for* good works (Eph. 2:10); but

---

[24] Greg L. Bahnsen, *By This Standard: The Authority of God's Law Today* (Powder Springs, GA: American Vision Press, 2008), 53. Emphasis Original.

don't forget that in order to do those good works, we need the truth that makes it function properly (Eph. 2:1-9).

## LIFE IN THE SPIRIT VS. LIFE IN THE FLESH

The Bible goes through great pains to articulate the difference between living in the Spirit and living in the flesh. One relies on the power of the gospel, while the other ignores the gospel and relies on self. The Apostle Paul lays this out for us,

> There is therefore now no condemnation for those who are in Christ Jesus. For the law of the Spirit of life has set you free in Christ Jesus from the law of sin and death. For God has done what the law, weakened by the flesh, could not do. By sending his own Son in the likeness of sinful flesh and for sin, he condemned sin in the flesh, in order that the righteous requirement of the law might be fulfilled in us, who walk not according to the flesh but according to the Spirit. For those who live according to the flesh set their minds on the things of the flesh, but those who live according to the Spirit set their minds on the things of the Spirit. —Romans 8:1-5

The work of the Holy Spirit is necessary for sanctification. Because of the objective removal of condemnation brought about by Christ in response to our depravity, certain things are now true. Paul says that we are set free from the law's consequences (sin and death) by new life wrought in us by the Spirit. Jesus' vicarious, penal substitutionary death described in verses three to four makes life in the Spirit a new reality in which believers function. The outworking of the gospel of Jesus is applied to the believer through the power of the Spirit who then draws them back full circle to the gospel. Yes, as pointed out a minute ago, the dominion of sin is over. But it still wages guerrilla warfare against us (Rom. 7:20). So what do we do? Set the mind on the Spirit.

Flesh brings death, destruction, sin, guilt, and shame. The Spirit brings life, new construction, freedom from sin, and the removal of guilt and shame. The flesh wants to be a law unto itself. The Spirit desires to produce Godly affections in obedience to God's law. Life in the Spirit isn't just better pragmatically, it's better because the news is *good*. John Owen comments,

> We are told to 'walk in the Spirit' (Gal. 5:16). This is to walk in obedience to God in dependence on the supplies of grace which the Holy Spirit gives us. If we walk in the Spirit we shall 'not fulfill the lusts of the flesh'. This can only mean that we shall be kept by the Spirit in holy obedience and enabled by the same Spirit to avoid sin. We are said to be 'let by the Spirit' (Gal. 5:18). This means that we are so worked on and influenced by the Spirit as to be kept from being worked on and influenced by vicious, depraved principles arising from our corrupt nature . . . To walk after the flesh is to have the principle of indwelling sin working in us to produce actual sins. So, to walk according to the Spirit is to have the Spirit working in us to produce all holy activities and duties.[25]

The Christian who has the work of the indwelling Spirit is set apart as holy, and demanded to be holy. The heart, in its misery, is useless apart from the regenerating power of a new conversion. Once freed from its insistence on disobedience, the Holy Spirit (there is a reason He is called "Holy"!) works to sanctify the believer's heart and mind by renewing him with the objective truths of the gospel. The power for sanctification is the gospel of Christ and the work of the Holy Spirit. The pattern for sanctification is the law. The purpose of sanctification is to be holy. Yes, indeed, the law is powerless to save. But thanks be to God our Father for sending His beloved Son to not only defeat death, but give us His very Spirit to enable us to walk in obedience.

---

[25] John Owen, *The Holy Spirit*, abridged and simplified by R.J.K. Law (Edinburgh: Banner of Truth, 2012), 159.

## GRACE-DRIVEN, GOSPEL FUELED WORK

God is committed to your sanctification. He doesn't just save you then walk away saying, "Good luck." He is actively at work in your life sanctifying you in truth through the word of God (Jn. 17:17). The charge that obedience inherently means legalism is unwarranted. The belief that man is a law unto himself is deplorable. So what happens, next?

If the heart is central to the human experience, then it follows that obedience to God's commands must start there. But is that where it ends? Greg Bahnsen says that, "Obedience must be from the heart, and yet that obedience must not be restricted to the heart."[26] Far too much of Christian thinking has been reduced to simple obedience to the heart. In an effort to forgive someone who wronged them, people will say things like, "His heart was in the right place," or "He has a great heart." It must start there, for sure, but it cannot end there. Obedience is required in our *actions*, not just our *intentions*. There are far-reaching consequences for God's law, both in the realm of the Church, the State, and the Family. To truncate the work of the gospel in our life by restricting it to the heart is dangerous.

Sanctification is grace-driven, gospel-fueled *work*. It takes physical, emotional and mental energy. It takes time to diligently search the Scriptures so we can have life (Jn. 5:39-40). It takes effort that is birthed out of an adequate knowledge of the gospel. You see, sanctification is becoming who we already are (1 Cor. 7:17). Sanctification is driven by past, present, and future justification as well as Jesus and His promises. It works when we *know* the penalty of sin has been paid for us. It's knowing the gospel frees us from the power of sin in our life as well as the presence of sin in the future. Sanctification is more than, though certainly not any less than, familiarizing ourselves with the beauty of justification. It's grabbing ahold of Jesus himself and striving to be in His image as the Spirit carves the gospel in our soul.

---

[26] Greg L. Bahnsen, *By This Standard: The Authority of God's Law Today* (Powder Springs, GA: American Vision Press, 2008), 25.

Regeneration is the new birth with a new heart; justification is the new status with the Judge of the universe; adoption is the new family. It follows that sanctification is the new growth with new affection from that new heart, new motivations from our new legal status, and new accountability from the new family. All of this for the glory of the Father, through the work of the Son, by the power of the Spirit.

However, it's not as though grace helps you get saved, and then sanctification becomes your own deal. Grace doesn't just help you along a little bit here and there; no, grace is what sustains you for everything all of the time. The confusion of legalism and antinomianism is a devastating one. It has confused the law's role in the life of the believer, and it has conflated justification and sanctification. But being gospel-centered does not equal law-negating. Regardless of our own insufficiencies, the gospel gives us hope:

> Since then we have a great high priest who has passed through the heavens, Jesus, the Son of God, let us hold fast our confession. For we do not have a high priest who is unable to sympathize with our weaknesses, but one who in every respect has been tempted as we are, yet without sin. Let us then with confidence draw near to the throne of grace, that we may receive mercy and find grace to help in time of need. —Hebrews 4:14-16

Salvation is of the Lord! We have a High Priest who has done the work for us, and now we can approach Him with a confident boldness, knowing that He will not turn us away. If the High Priest says it, then it is true.

One of the most common enemies of grace today is moralism (we will revisit this later). Moralism is like paddling upstream in a raging Colorado river with a Q-tip. Trying to pursue moralism for the sake of moralism is futile. If growth is going to happen, the proper fuel (gospel) must be in the engine. If in preaching, for example, the law is proclaimed and the gospel left behind, the direct result is moralism. Moralism infects the church today. I raise this issue briefly to say this: gospel preaching, and gospel-driven, gospel-fueled work requires repentance. And repentance requires law.

Biblical repentance is being more impressed with Christ's performance—His active and passive obedience[27]—than your own weak attempts. Many Christians are more obsessed with what they've done for Jesus than what He has done for them. Sanctification requires we take our eyes off ourselves and put them on Jesus.

It's not legalism to obey. Obedience is the result of a heart changed towards the things of God. We do not rely on moralism nor do we fall into the trap of legalism or antinomianism, but instead we cherish deeply the all-encompassing, God-glorifying gospel of our Lord Jesus Christ. The gospel isn't just good news yesterday—it's good news now, and it will still be good news tomorrow.

---

[27] Christ's active obedience refers to His keeping of the law and obedience to the Father. His passive obedience refers to His death and resurrection, suffering the penalty of our sin on our behalf.

CHAPTER FOUR

# MAKE WAR

Up to this point, we have done a lot of reconnaissance work. We've scouted the terrain, surveyed the main themes, and now we must do battle.

If we are going to make, mature, and multiply disciples of Jesus Christ then we must equip our soldiers with appropriate tools to do battle. Soldiers who are unequipped or even ill-equipped with no tools, or faulty tools, will do great harm to themselves and others. If we as disciples who make other disciples (this is, after all, our commission) are going to win the battle against the flesh and the enemy, we must make war.

## TOOLS OF THE TRADE

One of my favorite passages of Scripture is Ephesians 6:10-20:

> Finally, be strong in the Lord and in the strength of his might. Put on the whole armor of God, that you may be able to stand against the schemes of the devil. For we do not wrestle against flesh and blood, but against the rulers, against the authorities, against the cosmic powers over this present darkness, against the spiritual forces of evil in the heavenly places. Therefore take up the whole armor of God, that you may be able to withstand in the evil day, and having done all, to stand firm. Stand therefore, having fastened on the belt of truth, and having put on the breastplate of righteousness, and, as shoes for your feet, having put on the readiness given by the gospel of peace. In all circumstances

> take up the shield of faith, with which you can extinguish all the flaming darts of the evil one; and take the helmet of salvation, and the sword of the Spirit, which is the word of God, praying at all times in the Spirit, with all prayer and supplication. To that end keep alert with all perseverance, making supplication for all the saints, and also for me, that words may be given to me in opening my mouth boldly to proclaim the mystery of the gospel, for which I am an ambassador in chains, that I may declare it boldly, as I ought to speak.

The Apostle Paul is *not* saying that we wrestle *only* against rulers, authorities, and cosmic powers, but that those powers are the *bigger picture*. This passage is a call to arms—a call to do battle against the enemy. Like a general getting his soldiers ready, so Paul wishes to get the Church ready for war. The entire metaphor is built around the Spirit's work of providing protection for us on our way to glorification.

First, he says that we are to be strong "in the Lord." There is much in the world to drive us to despair, so we need strength in God, not in self or anyone else. Christ *has* called us to do good works (Eph. 2:10), and we have access to the Father by the power of the Spirit through the work of Christ (2:18). The road won't be easy, since we have to walk as wise people, not unwise people (3:15), knowing that evil abounds (3:16). There's much at stake in this battle of sanctification. The enemy is real.

Part of what the Apostle Paul is getting at in this passage is that, yes, strength resides in the Lord (vs. 10), and because of that truth, we can be strong in His might, and stand firm (vs. 13). "Strong," "strength," "might," "stand against," "wrestle," "armor"—these are all words that Paul uses to paint the picture. So what is the armor the helps us *do* those things?

Paul says to "take up the whole armor of God" (vs. 13)—not part of it, not some of it . . . all of it. A soldier who leaves behind part of his armor will be vulnerable. Paul starts the metaphor with the belt of truth because the word of truth is the gospel (Jn. 17:17). The gospel takes central stage because, like a belt, you need your armor to fit together properly on your body. Nothing works unless connected to the gospel. The belt holds everything together. More broadly, the belt holds the sword. Our confidence, then, is in the truthfulness of God's word; we can rely on it with complete faith, knowing that it will sustain us during war.

Paul goes on to describe these tools by telling us to having a breastplate of righteousness. The devil is a slanderer and wishes to inflict harm on our hearts. Because of the imputed righteousness of Christ (Rom. 4:6-11; Phil. 3:9), Christians can believe the truth of what the gospel teaches instead of the lies of the Liar who wishes to stab you in the heart with a false identity. What Paul is getting at is that because of Christ's righteousness given to us, we can withstand the attack on our identity by relying on the truth that our pursuit of righteousness is driven by Christ's righteousness given to us. The breastplate prevails against any effort of the enemy.

The next tool of the trade are shoes of peace. Paul has already alluded to Christ being our peace (2:14), Christ's work as the fulfillment of the temple sacrifices, thus making peace for us with the Father (2:15), and Christ's preaching of peace to those far off (Gentiles) and those near (Jews), in fulfillment of Isaiah 57:19 (cf. Eph. 2:17). Peace is central to the gospel, for Christ's work on the cross brought reconciliation to sinners who were at enmity with God (2:1-3). Paul's allusion to shoes is certainly Isaiah's concern (52:7), and the apostle quotes that very verse in Romans 10:15. Like a Roman soldier with tightened straps on his sandals, so is a Christian who walks in the peace of God offered in the gospel. In battle, we need this stability in our feet.

Paul goes on to tell us to take up the shield of faith (vs. 16). In the ancient times, particularly for the Romans, the shield was big enough to cover the entire body. Faith does that for the Christian. Faith covers everything as it works to defend any attack from the opposing army. Though the enemy will send flaming darts, a shield protects against those attacks. The apostle John says it best:

> For everyone who has been born of God overcomes the world. And this is the victory that has overcome the world—our faith. —1 John 5:4

J.C. Ryle says that, *"Habitual lively faith in Christ's presence and readiness to help* is the secret of the Christian soldier fighting successfully."[28] Faith overcomes.

The helmet of salvation is our next piece of equipment (vs. 17). Paul understands the past, present, and future nature of salvation (2:8; cf. 1 Thess. 5:8). The penalty has been paid, the power of sin is currently being subdued, and the future of the gospel at work will be a complete removal of sin from the planet. Salvation protects the head from thinking that any attack from the evil one will result in a change of mind. We have been given the mind of Christ (1 Cor. 2:16). Protect it with the assurance and security of our salvation (Eph. 1:14).

It is impossible to win a battle when always in defense mode. Offensive strikes must take place if a Christian is going to make war on sin. Thus Paul tells us to take up the sword of the Spirit, the word of God (vs. 17). The word of God is sharp enough to cut to the bone (Heb. 4:12). Its precision is unmatched; its immutability unwavering. The word of God destroys all attempts of the enemy. When tempted by the Liar, Jesus uses Scripture to attack him (Matt. 4:1-11). Memorizing, studying, reading, contemplating, speaking, and learning God's word is absolutely essential for the war. Use it often.

The equipment has been issued. The final call to battle is a call to militant prayer. Prayer is God's means to shape His warriors. Prayer is a call to keep alert and persevere (vs. 18); praying for your friends, so that the gospel can be proclaimed boldly (vs. 19). Prayer is an admission that you are powerless to uphold and control your world. Militant prayer is for those who are needy—needy for the Lord of Glory to fight for us. These are the tools of the trade. If we are to make war on sin, we must prayerfully use this equipment.

---

[28] J.C. Ryle, *Holiness: It's Nature, Hindrances, Difficulties, and Roots* (Peabody, MA: Hendrickson Publishers, Inc., 2007), 74. Emphasis in the original.

## WHAT'S YOUR ATTITUDE?

What is your attitude towards sin? Be honest. It does no good to equip yourself with these tools if you don't see yourself in a battle. Putting down the sword, taking of the helmet, kicking your feet up on the ottoman, and loosing your belt are all signs of an attitude of peace-time thinking. This is war time, not peace time. The enemy is relentless, your flesh is persistent, and the urgency behind this battle bar none. We cannot take our hand off the plow (Lk. 9:62).

Paul writes elsewhere:

> Put to death therefore what is earthly in you: sexual immorality, impurity, passion, evil desire, and covetousness, which is idolatry. On account of these the wrath of God is coming. In these you too once walked, when you were living in them. But now you must put them all away: anger, wrath, malice, slander, and obscene talk from your mouth. Do not lie to one another, seeing that you have put off the old self with its practices and have put on the new self, which is being renewed in knowledge after the image of its creator. — Colossians 3:5-10

Once again we have an imperative that follows the preceding indicative (vs. 1-4). Paul commands the Church to "put [sin] to death." Don't toy with it, kill it. We've already touched on this issue of mortification, but it is worth repeating—*to mortify sin requires an attitude towards sin that is nothing short of violent*.

Sin is not a force to be reasoned with, nor a thing to make peace with. Sin must be destroyed. There is no way to rationalize it, or make friends with it. Sin is destructive and tenacious in its destruction. Our attitude towards sin is not to cuddle with it, but be aggressively violent towards it. If sin is waging a war against us, why wouldn't we wage war in response? "The prudent sees danger and hides himself, but the simple go on and suffer for it" (Prov. 27:12).

There are many ways in which we shrink God's holiness and simultaneously increase our pride. All of it stems from our attitudes towards sin. We hide our sin—concealing the bad stuff in our lives from those around us for fear of what others might think about us. We become fake because of sin—meaning that we want to impress others, so we put on the mask and pretend we do not have sin in our lives. One of the major ways in which we function in minimizing our sin is blaming it on others, or explaining it away. This is the result of someone who downplays the seriousness of the crime. When we blame others ("Satan made me do it!"), we are *not* waging war, but instead acting like there isn't one, and that it isn't against us. Blaming stems from a heart that cannot own its shortcomings and reacts by defending itself. The heart's natural propensity when confronted with sin is to go into defense mode. Instead of allowing room for the flesh to justify itself, make war, using the equipment described above to "put to death" those sins that dwell inside of you. This comes from the motivation of godly sorrow (2 Cor. 7:8-10). It ought to make us happy to put sin to death, for we dare not offend our Maker.

One of the major problems in Christian thinking today is that many have bought into the "self-help" movement. Since we are talking about attitudes and ways we minimize sin in our lives, this is important to discuss. The "Christian" self-help movement perpetuates the idea that since the problem isn't inside of you (your heart), the solution must be you, because, let's face it, the world is a jerk and you could do no harm. Instead of owning sin, the attitude becomes virtual complete denial of indwelling sin, and instead of the cross being the central focus, the self becomes the central focus.

The problem with self-reflection in sanctification is that you never get around to looking at Christ. The scorecard is whatever you deem it: good feelings, favorable circumstances, blessings that outweigh negative things, and strong self-esteem. If the gospel is about what has happened inside of you, not the objective doctrine of Christ (which originates *outside* of you), then it's not the gospel! In other words, people think that the gospel itself is what is inside of you; therefore, if things go well, then the gospel is great. If things go bad, well, then I'm not trying hard enough. Those who insist on the belief that Jesus did His work, now I'll do mine, are holding fast not to the Word, but to the self. Self-reflection can be helpful, but on its own it does harm.

Which means that humility must take precedence in the life of a believer. Jonathan Edwards comments:

> A truly humble man is sensible of the small extent of his own knowledge, and the great extent of his ignorance, and of the small extent of his understanding as compared with the understanding of God. He is sensible of his weakness; how little his strength is, and how little he is able to do. He is sensible of his natural distance from God; of his dependence on him; of the insufficiency of his own power and wisdom; and that it is by God's power that he is upheld and provided for, and that he needs God's wisdom to lead and guide him, and his might to enable him to do what he ought to do for him.[29]

Humility is the cultivation of the gospel in the life of a believer. The gospel humbles a man, but does not strike him down in despair. The gospel also exalts a man, but does not lift him into pride. Your attitude towards sin is directly proportionate to your time spent reveling in the good news of Christ. The call is to make war, putting sin to death. Work out your salvation with fear and trembling, putting to death the old Adamic nature inside. But we do not wield our weaponry with arrogance, but with humility. So, what's your attitude? If it's anything short of 1 John 3:9-10, then we have a problem:

> No one born of God makes a practice of sinning, for God's seed abides in him, and he cannot keep on sinning because he has been born of God. By this it is evident who are the children of God, and who are the children of the devil: whoever does not practice righteousness is not of God, nor is the one who does not love his brother.

[29] Jonathan Edwards, *Charity and Its Fruits* (Edinburgh: Banner of Truth, 2005), 133.

## PREACHING THE GOSPEL

We have the tools and know the motives, but how do we do it? By preaching the gospel to ourselves, and to one another.

"What you really need is good news," I told him. He didn't understand. We had met time and time again and unknowingly, he was trying to perform his way into the kingdom. "You can't do that," I exhorted. "Otherwise you miss the entire point of Jesus and His performance on your behalf!"

Whether we acknowledge it or not, we all need good news. Not just good news, but *better-than-anything news*. News that announces something spectacular—like nothing you could ever imagine or fabricate. And until you recognize this need, you'll be helpless. Like an engine with no gas, your life, without a constant barrage of Jesus-is-King news, will stall.

I often tell my congregation that I have thirty-four years left in my ministry here, and for those thirty-four years, you will hear the gospel over and over again, not because you don't know it in your brain, but because knowing it in your brain isn't enough. We must know it—*I* must know it—in our hearts, and in our hands. Remember, the gospel isn't the starting point—it *is* the point. It's the point of everything! And until we understand this truth, we will continue to be lured away, enticed by other false gospels that over-promise and underdeliver. These things distract us from making war.

Martin Luther is reported to have said that he continues to preach the gospel each and every week because each and every week his people forget it. I'm sure he would include himself in this assertion because let's face it, we're all guilty as charged.

Because of this, there are five simple reasons why we need to hear about Jesus and His glorious gospel each and every day. "Give us Jesus" ought to be the rally cry of the church. If we are to make war, we must do so here. Over and over again, our hearts should be yearning to hear the gospel again and again—like my two-year-old daughter begging for a "horsey-ride" on my back, let us go back to the truth that sets us free. We make war using the preaching of the gospel to ourselves and each other:

## 1. So Our Affections Are Stirred

Our emotions are impressed with many things. Whether a good movie, television show, football game, or shiny new Apple product, we love an emotionally stirring experience. We thrive on it. But what happens when those emotions become sour? What happens when we just don't feel like worshiping Jesus and finding joy in him? What do you do when your affections are clouded with bitterness, jealousy, envy, and anger? What happens in war if you are tired and just don't "feel it"?

Jonathan Edwards is helpful: "Upon the whole, I think it is clearly manifest, that all truly gracious affections arise from special and peculiar influences of the Spirit, working that *sensible effect* or *sensation* in the souls of the saints."[30]

It is the Holy Spirit that drives our affections towards gospel holiness and one of the means by which He does so is through gospel proclamation. We need it. Fighting for joy is absolutely that—a fight; but joy in Him is absolutely worth it (Ps. 16:11). Only when old affections have been expunged by greater, far superior affections can we be free from idolatry.

You see, in war time, your affections can take a beating. You can be side-tracked by other things. You don't have time to sit around and worry about those distractions. Making war is an all-out declaration that the only thing that matters in this moment, at this time, is that the gospel takes precedence against the enemy. You will feel overwhelmed. God gives you more than you can handle because the idol of self-sufficiency is destructive. You can't make your heart feel good towards God. You need something from the outside, namely, good news. The gospel stirs up affections, like bubbles in a glass jar, so that what comes out of you is holy.

## 2. So Our Identities Are Clarified

Whether it is a counseling appointment with a young man trying to understand what he should do with his life, or a newly engaged couple looking for some premarital help, I am con-

---

[30] Jonathan Edwards, *The Works of Jonathan Edwards, Volume 1* (Bellingham, WA: Logos Bible Software, 2008). 267. Emphasis in the original.

vinced that the root issue with all of our problems is an issue of identity. For example, no matter the marital issue, I can always trace the issue between the husband and wife back to the problem of a husband not being a biblical husband, and a wife not being a biblical wife. Identity matters tremendously.

If you think about it—sin is a loss of identity. When Adam and Eve sinned against God in the garden, they lost their identity as a covenant people with their covenant God. Subsequently, because of their transgression, their lives were marred by sin and ever since then, man, made in God's image, has simply forgotten who he is in relationship to God. Everyone knows He exists (Rom. 1:20); however, the issue is identity amnesia.

Take the example of the pursuit of holiness. For the Christian, the battle of sanctification is a battle to be who you are. If you're a redeemed saint, then act like one! When we give ourselves to sin, we lose our identity—hence the need for the gospel. We need a constant reminder that we are freely justified in Christ to rest in Him. Wartime has a tendency to distract us, so it is important to know who you are.

## 3. So Our Idols Are Uprooted

John Calvin wrote, "The human mind is, so to speak, a perpetual forge of idols."[31] Calvin was on to something. Every time we lose sight of the gospel it is because we have taken our eyes away from Jesus and placed them on an idol. Idols can be subversively deceptive, or they can be patently obvious. Either way, this side of glorification will undoubtedly be marked by a constant fight with idols. That's what happens in war.

An idol cannot be uprooted by mere moral effort. It has to be uprooted and replaced by something far superior, namely, the gospel. And what better way to see an idol uprooted, than the goodness of the good news? The intensity of pain we feel when an idol is removed from us is directly proportionate to how far away we walked from belief in the gospel. If sin and idolatry is trusting, confiding, believing, and gaining identity

---

[31] John Calvin, *Institutes of the Christian Religion* (Peabody, MA: Hendrickson Publishers, Inc., 2008), 55.

from something other than God, then it follows that we ought to, through repentance and faith, trust, confide, believe, and gain our identity in Jesus. Idols are destroyed when good news is heeded.

## 4. So Our Covenant Is Kept

As talked about in the previous chapter, the New Covenant instituted by our Lord is meant to be kept. Sometimes we do not often talk like this, mostly because in portions of our culture we've lost the key concepts behind covenant. Regardless of unconscious ignorance, it is our duty—indeed it is commanded of us!—to "be holy" (1 Pt. 1:15-16; cf. Lev. 11:44). To be sure, Christ is our wisdom, righteousness, sanctification, and redemption (1 Cor. 1:30). However, we are still called to the covenant obligations of obedience. And because of the indwelling power of God the Holy Spirit, we can follow Jesus in obedience (Jn. 14:21) because the law has been written on our hearts (Jer. 31:33; cf. 2 Cor. 3:6). This happens through the work of the Spirit leading us to truth (Jn. 17:17) and glorifying Christ (the power of the gospel in us). You need to hear it, because the Spirit uses it to drive your obedience.

## 5. So Our Mission Is Spurred On

So having had our affections stirred, our identities clarified, our idols uprooted, and our covenant in check, what do we do? The answer? Make disciples. This is our mission. The gospel is news; therefore, it should be proclaimed. Boldly, I might add. After all, Jesus has been given all authority—we need not fear (Matt. 28:18; more on this in the next chapter).

If we do not continue to go back to the good news again and again, we will lose sight of our identity, and purpose. The gospel is the engine that drives this whole thing. Without it, we are lost. Again and again, we need to hear, see, believe, experience afresh, enjoy, and understand the good news of Jesus' work on our behalf: His virgin birth, His perfect life under the law of God, His perfect fulfillment of the Old Testament Scriptures (Israel's story), His substitutionary death, His resurrection, His ascension to the throne, and His current mediation—this is our gospel! Let it spur us on to do His work.

"I have stored up your word in my heart," the writer says, "that I might not sin against you" (Ps. 119:11). The issue is not just hearing the gospel, but marinating in it as well. Whether proclaimed from the pulpit or shared over a cup of coffee, the gospel must take center stage, because we do not want to sin against God. When it is stored in our hearts and minds, we get all of the benefits mentioned above. But the ultimate benefit is that we get God. We need the good news because we need God. The war against sin is not a war against sin *in and of itself*. The war against indwelling sin is a war to get God. He is the prize worth pursuing.

I close this chapter with a call to arms. Will you rest in the righteousness of Christ credited to your account? Will you walk in peace, knowing that peace is at the heart of gospel? Will you put on the helmet of salvation, knowing that your salvation has been secured because of Christ's perfect work? Will you tighten the belt of truth so that your life is held together by the truth of God's word? Will you hold fast and "contend for the faith that was once for all delivered to the saints" (Jude 1:3)? Will you boldly take up your sword, trust in the authority of Scripture, and wield it with humility? If so, then you *must* wage war knowing the battle has already been won. Christ is victorious. Christ is King.

## CHAPTER FIVE

# HOLINESS AND THE CHURCH

I made the argument in chapter 2 that the Church must revisit the doctrine of God and I would add to that the doctrine of the Church. There are no unimportant doctrines, but these two are crucial due to the pluralistic culture which in America we find ourselves in. Varying beliefs about "the man upstairs" permeates just about every cultural religious conviction it seems. God has become an abstract concept, an impersonal force behind nature, and an idea to whom we attribute certain things outside of ourselves because let's face it, everyone is spiritual, but not religious.

What I intend to accomplish in this chapter is fairly straightforward. I want us to explore how holiness is connected to the Church. Though not exhaustive by any means, we will investigate the implications of Christ's substitutionary death, and how His blood purchased a people for Himself. From here we will look at Christ's High Priestly prayer as Jesus asks that the Father allow His people to behold His glory. After this, my hope is to explore an understanding of missional holiness, and look at the marks of a Church that act as a foretaste of the heavenly kingdom.

## JESUS MAKES HIS CHURCH

It is only fitting that Jesus be worshiped as High Priest because He is the High Priest—the Lamb of God who takes away sin (Jn. 1:29). Jesus' work on the cross was the fulfillment of the Levitical priesthood as He made atonement for His people by offering Himself as a sacrifice to end all sacrifices (Heb. 9:11-28; cf. Lev. 16). A survey of sanctification would not be possible without the cross of Christ--the zenith of our Priest's sacrificial work.

One often-overlooked passage in Scripture is Ephesians 2:11-22. It's overlooked because the famous "grace through faith" passage (Eph. 2:1-10) precedes it and is a treasure chest full of gospel goodness. But to ignore the rest of Paul's thought would fail to do justice to his entire argument. Before we look at verses 11-22, we need to remember the context. Paul begins the chapter by reminding the Gentiles that they were dead in their trespasses and sins and unable to change their own hearts (2:1). They walked in whatever passions they pleased, and were by nature, "children of wrath" (vs. 3). They, as well as the rest of mankind, deserved nothing but judgment for their sin. However, verse 4 changes everything. God shows mercy by making us alive by grace through faith—both gifts from God—in order to show "the immeasurable riches of his grace toward us in Christ Jesus" (vs. 7). It is nothing we did that merited God's favor, it's what God does that restores a person at enmity with God to a position of peace with God.

Paul warns the Gentiles not to forget this:

> Therefore remember that at one time you Gentiles in the flesh, called "the uncircumcision" by what is called the circumcision, which is made in the flesh by hands—remember that you were at that time separated from Christ, alienated from the commonwealth of Israel and strangers to the covenants of promise, having no hope and without God in the world. But now in Christ Jesus you who once were far off have been brought near by the blood of Christ. For he himself is our peace, who has made us both one and has broken down in his flesh the dividing wall of hostility by abolishing the law of commandments expressed in ordinances, that he might create in himself one new man in

> place of the two, so making peace, and might reconcile us both to God in one body through the cross, thereby killing the hostility. And he came and preached peace to you who were far off and peace to those who were near. For through him we both have access in one Spirit to the Father. So then you are no longer strangers and aliens, but you are fellow citizens with the saints and members of the household of God, built on the foundation of the apostles and prophets, Christ Jesus himself being the cornerstone, in whom the whole structure, being joined together, grows into a holy temple in the Lord. In him you also are being built together into a dwelling place for God by the Spirit. —Ephesians 2:11-22

This new "household of God" is none other than the "Israel of God" (Gal. 6:16). Because of God's saving righteous activity in the gospel (Rom. 1:16-17), Gentiles are now grafted together with the remnant of believing Jews to form a New Covenant People of God (Rom. 11:11-24). There is continuity that must be acknowledged. Christ didn't come to abolish the Law and the Prophets (Matt. 5:17), but instead came to fulfill them by *bringing God's restorative plan of salvation to the nations.*[32]

There is only one people of God, not two. Gentiles have been brought in when they were "far off" (vs. 17). Both the Jew and the Gentile (the Church collectively) have access to the Father "in one Spirit" (vs. 18). Because of this, Gentiles are no longer strangers and aliens but are "fellow citizens with the saints and members of the household of God" (vs. 19), Christ now being the cornerstone (vs. 20). What's the basis for all of this? "But now in

---

[32] While I do not have the time to get into this, we must remember that this was always the goal of God: the nations. He intended for Israel to do the same, "I am the Lord; I have called you in righteousness; I will take you by the hand and keep you; I will give you as a covenant for the people, *a light for the nations,* to open the eyes that are blind, to bring out the prisoners from the dungeon, from the prison those who sit in darkness" (Isaiah 42:6-7).

Christ Jesus you who once were far off have been brought near by the blood of Christ" (vs. 13).

This is why the Apostle Paul can say, "You are not your own, for you were bought with a price" (1 Cor. 6:19-20). Sin held man captive, but Christ's sacrifice ransomed him back out of the slave market of sin. The blood of Christ takes away sin, but not without cost. It cost Jesus His life to make for Himself a forgiven people. The perfect, spotless Lamb made a perfect atonement (Exod. 12:5; cf. Lev. 9:3).

The atonement made by Christ bought this peace and brought us together in an inseparable union. His sacrifice is explained in the upper room story in Matthew 26:26-28:

> Now as they were eating, Jesus took bread, and after blessing it broke it and gave it to the disciples, and said, "Take, eat; this is my body." And he took a cup, and when he had given thanks he gave it to them, saying, "Drink of it, all of you, for this is my blood of the covenant, which is poured out for many for the forgiveness of sins."

The Church has been ransomed, bought with the blood of Christ, which resulted in a perfect covenant union. Oh, precious is the flow! Because we have been purchased, we are no longer slaves to sin, but instead slaves to Christ. And the beauty is, He's given us a new heart that wants to be His slave. Jesus is making His Church, and hell doesn't stand a chance (Matt. 16:18).

My prayer is that we do not over-familiarize ourselves with the beauty of this covenant union. There is a danger in assuming too much. A simple glance at Ephesians helps us see the depths of being "in Christ." In fact, Paul's entire theology regarding union with Christ is built on a robust understanding of the covenant union between Jesus and His Church. For example, Paul explains that the Gentiles have been redeemed by Christ's blood because "now" they are "in Christ Jesus" (Eph. 2:13). Before that, Paul demonstrated that they were "created in Christ Jesus" to do good works (vs. 10), thus proving the spiritual aspect of this objective reality and union. Kevin DeYoung is helpful here,

> Apart from our union with Christ every effort to imitate Christ, no matter how noble and inspired at the outset, inevitably leads to legalism and spiritual defeat. But once you understand the doctrine of union with Christ, you see that God doesn't ask us to attain to what we're not. He only calls us to accomplish what already is. The pursuit of holiness is not a quixotic effort to do just what Jesus did. It's the fight to live out the life that has already been made alive in Christ.[33]

I should hasten to say that an accurate understanding of the gospel leads to an accurate understanding of the Church. The reason is, that many of us know the *individual* pieces of the gospel, but we oftentimes forget the *corporate* pieces of the gospel. In other words, Paul has just laid out the magnificent truths of the gospel, and, not only can our sins be forgiven by the work of our High Priest, we have been (past tense) made alive! And not just made alive, made alive *together* as His people! DeYoung is right. God doesn't ask any of us to try and reach something that we'll never reach, or attain something we'll never attain. God asks us to live our lives (imperatives) as though these realities (indicatives) are true *because they are true*. Union with Christ is an important theology, because apart from Christ, we can do nothing (Jn. 15:5).

Jesus makes His Church with His very own life, death, resurrection, ascension, and mediation. And to His mediation we must now turn.

## JESUS PRAYS FOR HIS CHURCH

One of the most powerful sections of Scripture is found in John chapter 17. Jesus doesn't just make His Church, He prays for her as well. Intercession on behalf of His people isn't just something He did once, but something He continues to do (Heb. 7:25). Perhaps a brief refresher on the structure of the chapter as well as the context leading up to this chapter will help.

---

[33] Kevin DeYoung, *The Hole in Our Holiness: Filling the Gap Between Gospel Passion and the Pursuit of Godliness* (Wheaton, IL: Crossway, 2012), 100.

To start, Christ prays for Himself (vs. 1-5), then His disciples (vs. 6-19); after this, He prays for those who will boldly follow after Him in faith (vs. 20-26). This prayer is on the heels of saying to His disciples that He has "overcome the world" (Jn. 16:33). Jesus said a lot of hard things, and many people couldn't handle it (e.g., Jn. 6:66). His ministry to Israel had been rejected. He found a joyless nation without wine (2:1-12), a temple without authentic worship and prayer (2:13-22), a leader without a new birth (3:1-15), a woman at the well without accurate knowledge and worship (4:1-42), a set of Jewish leaders who were orphans (5:18), a nation hungry for only the tangible (6:1-5; 22-71), a nation called to be a light, but instead remained in darkness (8:12-59), and sheep without a shepherd (10:1-18).

Before Jesus prays, He raises His friend Lazarus from the dead with a simple command (11:1-44), receives an anointing by Mary (12:1-8), enters Jerusalem triumphantly (12:12-19), washes the feet of His disciples (13:1-20), gives a new commandment, which is really a recapitulation of the old ones (13:31-35), prophetically prepares a place (14:11-14), promises that the Spirit will come and be a Helper (14:15-31), reconstitutes Israel around Himself as the True Vine which requires constant abiding (15:1-27), discusses the work of the Holy Spirit (16:1-15), and promises that the disciples' sorrow will turn to joy in due time (16:16-24).

Now Jesus prays.

Jesus begins by asking the Father to "glorify [the] Son that the Son may glorify [the Father]" (17:1). The mutual glory-giving of the Trinity involves Jesus demonstrating to the world His obedience, and in that obedience, the Father is glorified. In turn, Jesus' death, resurrection, and enthronement serve as the Father's way of glorifying the Son. Jesus knows that His work has been accomplished (vs. 4), and He asks that the Father glorify Him "in [the Father's] own presence with the glory that [Jesus] had with [the Father] before the world existed" (vs. 5). But Jesus' work wasn't *entirely* over. He had to face that hill, knowing that there is no kingdom without a cross. Jesus is the "Christ," or "Messiah," the anointed son of man from Daniel 7 who would come to the Ancient of Days to inherit His kingdom

(Ps. 72:8; 110:1). Once this happens, the promises of the age to come will be realized, and the new creation project will begin. This is truly eternal life. Jesus has kept the Father's word (vs. 6), given the Father's words (vs. 8), and now prays, not for the world, but for those to whom the Father has given Him.

Jesus' prayer was one of protection. He knows that He is about to leave and go to the Father, but He asks that His people not be taken out of the world, but instead be protected from the evil one (vs. 15). Jesus asks that they be protected by the truth, as the Spirit works to sanctify them in truth in accordance to the Father's provision (vs. 17). The Father sent Jesus into the world, and now Jesus sends His disciples into the world (vs. 18). His prayer shifts a bit in verse 20, as He prays not only for those in His immediate possession, but those in the future who would believe. He prays that the Father would grant unity to His people, a unity that is reflected in the infinite bond of trinitarian love. Then Jesus says something bold in verse 24:

> Father, I desire that they also, whom you have given me, may be with me where I am, to see my glory that you have given me because you loved me before the foundation of the world.

The glory of Christ is the aim of Christ—its display and magnification, its treasuring in, delighting in, and basking in. The glory of Christ is the central prayer for Christ's Church. If holiness is full completion and restoration in *glorification*, it follows then that the process of sanctification terminates on the glory of Christ *here and now*. John Owen comments twice:

> One of the greatest privileges the believer has, both in this world and for eternity, is to behold the glory of Christ.[34]

[34] John Owen, *The Glory of Christ*, abridged and simplified by R.J.K. Law (Edinburgh: Banner of Truth, 2009), 2.

> No man shall ever behold the glory of Christ by sight in heaven who does not, in some measure, behold it by faith in this world.[35]

Jesus doesn't just pray that His people would see His glory from a distance, but that they would behold His glory now *and* in the future kingdom. The glory seen in Jesus' earthly life was His office of Messiah, His acts of mercy, and His obedience to the Father. Jesus' glory is His infinite worth and intrinsic value. For something or someone to have glory is for that object or person to hold weight and supremacy. Jesus holds all weight, all value, and all supremacy.

In Jewish thought, glory was connected to light. When God manifested himself, His light, radiance, and glory was so intense that a person would die if he came too close. In fact, God's presence and even a fraction of His glory has caused men to reconsider their disposition. In the garden, Adam and Eve hid themselves for fear of God (Gen. 3:8). Isaiah reassessed his own life after a confrontation with the glory of God (Is. 6:5). Some people tried to escape from the presence of God (Jn. 1:3), while others feared for their lives (Jgs. 13:22; Lk. 1:11-12; 2:9). The Scriptures also communicate quite frequently that when God reveals Himself to creation, everyone and everything trembles at His presence (Jgs. 5:5; Ps. 68:8; 97:4; 104:32; Is. 19:1; Nah. 1:5). The only adequate response to catching a glimpse of the bright and glorious light of God is fear (Jer. 5:22).

As Jesus prays for His Church, He prays that this same glory would be seen, but not just seen, delighted in also. This is the aim of the believer learning the path of sanctification. The goal of all Christians everywhere ought to be a beholding of the glory of Christ. John Owen beautifully adds to the discussion:

> It is by beholding the glory of Christ by faith that we are spiritually edified and built up in this world, for as we behold his glory, the life and power of faith grow stronger and stronger. It is by faith that we grow to love Christ. So if we desire strong faith and powerful love, which give us rest,

---

[35] Ibid., 4.

> peace and satisfaction, we must seek them by diligently beholding the glory of Christ by faith. In this duty I desire to live and to die. On Christ's glory I would fix all my thoughts and desires, and the more I see of the glory of Christ, the more the painted beauties of this world will wither in my eyes and I will be more and more crucified to this world. It will become to me like something dead and putrid, impossible for me to enjoy.[36]

We've talked a lot about the path and process of sanctification, the traps, the warnings, the motivations, the affections, and the demand to be holy. What we are getting into at this point is the object of all of those things. The object of our beholding is Jesus. It's not a concept about Jesus, truth about Jesus, or saying of Jesus, it's just Jesus, our Lord.

*Beholding leads to becoming.*

When our gaze is fixed upon the glory of Christ—His person, work, value, and truth—all other things, John Owen says, fade to the back and everything the world has to offer pales in comparison to the excellencies of Jesus Christ. This is partly what the apostle Paul is getting at in 2 Corinthians 3:18, when he writes:

> And we all, with unveiled face, beholding the glory of the Lord, are being transformed into the same image from one degree of glory to another. For this comes from the Lord who is the Spirit.

Paul says that the Spirit is the one who works in us to enable us to behold the glory of God, and that when we do the Spirit-empowered beholding, we are transformed into that same very image. In other words, sanctification is beholding, and beholding is becoming. Sanctification is being focused on Christ, and being focused on Christ is becoming like Him. Becoming like Christ is the aim of our sanctification. We want to act like He acts, think like He thinks, and do what He does. We want to imi-

---

36 Ibid., 7.

tate Him because we love Him. Beholding Christ is the means by which we become like Christ. May we, like Moses his encounter with God, reflect the glory of Christ in our countenance!

To behold the glory of Christ is fix all our attention, using all the faculties of our mind, affections, will, and thoughts, upon Christ. Every day while at work in front of our desk, every time we prepare a meal, every time we do laundry, every time we pray with someone, every time we tell someone about the glorious gospel of Jesus, every time we talk to our children, every time we pray with our children—every single moment of every single day is an opportunity to affix our gaze and attention on Christ. This is beholding. Beholding isn't looking for a moment at something then walking away unmoved. Beholding is an active fight to look at Christ long enough to enjoy that Person while every other trouble and anxiety we feel fades away in the distance.

This is Jesus' prayer for you. He prayed for you, that you would behold Him. That is not arrogant. It's not arrogant for the greatest source of pleasure in the universe to demand that you find happiness in Him. Christ loves His Church too much to let the degenerating pleasures of the world consume us, not when there is an infinite Treasure that awaits our beholding. We must fight to see and savor the excellencies of Christ. Owen masterfully comments again:

> One view of Christ's glory by faith will scatter all the fears, answer all the objections and disperse all the depressions of poor, tempted, doubting souls. To all believers it is an anchor which they may cast within the veil, to hold them firm and steadfast in all trials, storms and temptations, both in life and in death.[37]

Perhaps like the apostle John, we can say, "And the Word became flesh and dwelt among us, and *we have seen his glory*, glory as of the only Son from the Father, full of grace and truth" (Jn. 1:14). Our mediator has provided intercession for us, pray-

---

[37] Ibid., 81.

ing that we would see Him for who He really is. But He doesn't stop there.

## JESUS SENDS HIS CHURCH

The belief that someone can follow Jesus all by themselves (apart from a church) is imbecilic. No one functions at full capacity apart from the local church. If you're looking to destroy your sanctification, go ahead and sit at home listening to podcasts all by yourself. A cursory reading of Hebrews 10:19-39 will eliminate this view. Whether you know it or not, you *need* the local church. It's not because the local church needs something *from* you, but because *you are the Church*. The Church is *not* an activity, building, event or place—the Church is the people of God, the body of Christ, the bride of Christ, and *the means of Christ*.

Debate has ensued on what constitutes a church ever since the time of the apostles. What marks a church? How do we know? What means has Christ given to the church? These are great questions.

To start, the Church is both invisible and visible realities and signs. The *universal Church* is the elect of God from the beginning of time to the end of time; it is those whom God calls, "Mine." That is the invisible reality that only God can see.

However, there are visible realities and signs that help us know here in space and time what a church actually is. For example, a church is a local gathering of people under the Lordship of Christ and His gospel who proclaim His word, exercise church discipline per the instruction of our Lord, administer the sacraments of baptism and communion, and is governed by biblically qualified elders and deacons. Each of those aspects of a local church are to be pursued diligently with qualified men and women at the helm. Because of the nature of the covenant, the church uses these elements to help explain those invisible realities. That is how we know if something is a church. (I don't have the time to go into this too far, for it is well beyond the scope of this book.)

I mentioned a moment ago that the Church is the *means of Christ*. What I am saying is, the Church is God's set-apart people who live on mission, actively searching for ways to infiltrate the world with pockets of communities who proclaim the gospel, making disciples of Jesus, so that God's glory fills the earth (Ez. 43:2; Ps. 57:5; 72:19; Hab. 2:14). The gospel according to Matthew explains,

> And Jesus came and said to them, "All authority in heaven and on earth has been given to me. Go therefore and make disciples of all nations, baptizing them in the name of the Father and of the Son and of the Holy Spirit, teaching them to observe all that I have commanded you. And behold, I am with you always, to the end of the age." —Matt. 28:18-20

Jesus makes something very plain to us: *the Church is the means of Christ for displaying the worth of Christ to the nations of Christ.* Christ has all authority (Ps. 2; 110:1-2), and in that authority He sends His holy people to go and disciple the nations, baptizing them into the covenant of our Trinitarian God, teaching them God's Law as revealed in Christ Himself, and knowing that *He is with us.*

Don't miss what Jesus is getting at. Just as Jesus came to Israel, so the Church goes to the world. Jesus came to earth, formed a team of disciples (learners) and sends them out (cf. Jn. 20:21). We go to our neighborhoods, form teams of disciples (we call them Missional Communities), and send them out. *You can't do this by yourself.*

The path of sanctification isn't just about personal piety, it's about God's grand mission to restore all things to Himself. You and I get to play a role in the drama of life. This is missional holiness—living out the commands of God based upon the newfound realities of God as the Spirit works in us to make us holy. But is this a tension? Should we hide from the world and pietistically function as best we can in our private ways? Do we leave behind the pursuit of holiness in an effort to reach the world with the gospel? Yes, it's a tension. But we must do both.

In *Gospel-Centered Discipleship,* Jonathan Dodson explores this idea of missional holiness. He delineates between the natural pull of personal piety and the command to go and make disciples. What tends to happen for many people is a pull in one way or the other and some stronger than others. Some would prefer to keep to themselves and do their acts of piety alone with their Bible. But this person isn't doing mission. Others prefer to do mission, failing to remember that their identity in Christ is what fuels that mission. Thus the pendulum swing back-and-forth becomes impossible. Dodson clarifies:

> The gospel actually integrates piety and mission around a new gospel center. When the gospel is central to discipleship, our acceptance before God isn't performance based but grace based. The gospel frees us from running ragged trying to please God with holiness and social justice, because Jesus has pleased God for us and secured the mission. Jesus is tellings us to give up on our deeds and ourselves, and to give in to his deeds and him—as our Christ and as our Lord.[38]

What Dodson makes plain is that *sanctification is a both/and.* We are called to be holy and we *do* pursue holiness. We are called to make disciples and we do just that. But both of these only work when appropriated by the good news of Christ's work on our behalf. It's not a decision between personal piety and missional living, it's both. The reason it is important to discuss holiness and its inherent connection to the Church is because *the two things go hand-in-hand.* Holiness cannot be pursued apart from the mission of the Church, and the mission of the Church cannot be pursued without an understanding of holiness.

For example, discipleship is imitation. We are to imitate Christ. We do this in front of a watching world and it sometimes bothers us. Why? Maybe it's because we are afraid that people will see our true selves. But why should that matter? Do we not want people to see how desperately in need of the gospel we are? If we are to pursue what Christ has called us to do, we must understand who it is Christ has made us to be. This is the tension between holiness and Church.

---

[38] Jonathan K. Dodson, *Gospel-Centered Discipleship* (Wheaton, IL: Crossway, 2012), 47.

In the introduction I mentioned one of the struggles I had growing up as a Christian in the church was a defeatist eschatology. I do not mean that I thought the church would lose in the end times, but that the Christian life was so hard that it almost extinguished any amount of effort that I could muster. What's the point of pursuing Jesus if we're just sitting around waiting for Him to zap us off the planet? I didn't understand it. Yes, I had Rapture fever. I grew up in the *Left Behind* era. But what I didn't realize until a few years ago was that this outlook on life (particularly its view of the future) affected how I viewed the church, the mission, and holiness. Because my view of things was driven by a bleak hermeneutic, it rendered me helpless and incapacitated to want anything to do with holiness. This inadvertently caused a low view of the church, a low view of God's holiness, and with all of that a low view of Christ's work. Why pursue any of this if I'll never win?

Scripture says otherwise. "For he must reign until he has put all his enemies under his feet" (1 Cor. 15:25). To let the proverbial cat out of the bag, I'm a postmillennialist, which means that Jesus defeats all enemies and ultimately the gospel will triumph on earth before He returns. His Kingdom rule is a reality *now,* and it will grow to fill the earth (Dan. 2:36-45). But not only this, it means that *my pursuit of holiness on mission with Jesus will succeed because it is Christ who upholds me, not me and my faulty logic.* Christ has triumphed; death has been defeated, is being subdued, and will be damned forever: so why can't you pursue holiness?

God isn't asking us to pursue something we'll never reach. He's asking us to invest in something He's already accomplished. The Lamb has shed His blood, and He will provide His Father with a host of people who have been made pure forever, so that in eternity we will sing the chorus, "Holy, Holy, Holy."

Being missional (this is the "do" part of the Church that is fueled by the "be" part of our identity in Christ) means that we are relentless in our pursuit of the main goal, namely, seeing others enjoy God as much as we do. Jesus made His Church, prayed for His Church, and sent His Church, all for the glory of God, and the joy of man.

CHAPTER SIX

# HOLINESS AND JOY

Jonathan Edwards once wrote that, "Holiness and happiness are all one in heaven."[39] It's true. The treasure we receive after we have fought well in this life is the full consummation of holiness and joy. The two go hand-in-hand in the heavenly kingdom and the challenge for us in the here and now is the adequate cultivation of the two in our lives. The aim of this chapter is to examine holiness and joy. How do we cultivate holiness and joy? What's the relationship between the two? Does one take priority over another?

## THE RIGHT ORDER

The Puritan Richard Sibbes believes, "Those that look to be happy must first look to be holy."[40] This poses a problem for many Christians in America because the prevailing theological conviction is that God only exists to suit their needs in their timing. Personal pleasure is the object of desire—the end of blissful indulgence. "Unleash the inner champion inside of you because God just wants you to be happy" is the schtick. Of course, God wants you to be happy—*in Him*. But this man-centered thinking serves only to destroy a person's sanctification. Once the gospel

---

[39] Jonathan Edwards, *The Works of Jonathan Edwards, Volume 2*, (Bellingham, WA: Logos Bible Software, 2008), 618.

[40] Richard Sibbes, *The Golden Treasury of Puritan Quotations*, compiled by I.D.E. Thomas (Edinburgh: Banner of Truth, 2011), 158.

shifts to being about me and my own comfort (big house, new car, no suffering, etc.), it only makes sense that anything that gets in the way of my pursuit of pleasure in stuff be seen as a threat. This is partly what Martin Luther was getting at when he explored the difference between a theology of glory and the theology of the cross. The problem with all of this thinking is that it gets the order wrong. Sibbes was right. True happiness is only found when appropriated and fueled by holiness. Getting this order wrong is the difference between life and death, salvation and damnation.

Jesus provides a great illustration of getting the order right,

> Therefore, since we are surrounded by so great a cloud of witnesses, let us also lay aside every weight, and sin which clings so closely, and let us run with endurance the race that is set before us, looking to Jesus, the founder and perfecter of our faith, who for the joy that was set before him endured the cross, despising the shame, and is seated at the right hand of the throne of God. —Hebrews 12:1-2

The author of Hebrews is coming off the heels of the great "hall of faith" chapter. Faith is seen all over the pages of the Old Testament and because of it, the author encourages us to run with endurance. The just live by faith and so ought we because we are justified! We are to "lay aside every weight and sin" so that in running we can look to Jesus, keep our eye on the prize, and run *efficiently*. A runner can't win sitting down, nor can he race with a snow suit on. He must cast those things aside, stay diligent in his effort, and *keep going*. Who's the pattern for this? Jesus.

Jesus got the order right. He laid aside every weight, refused to sin (Heb. 4:15), and looked to the joy that was set *before* Him. Jesus didn't pursue joy in the things of this world, but in what was set before Him. What was before Him was the task of obedience which required a cross (coupled with shame), and the end result was a glorious exaltation to the throne (Dan. 2:44:45; 7:13-14; cf. Acts 1:9). He is our example and we must imitate Him (Jn. 13:15). The joy that is set before believers is a fullness of joy in His presence (Ps. 16:11). How do we get there? Holiness. Lay aside the weight. Lay aside the sin. Endure suffering like our brother, Jesus, who adopted us into the family and because of Him we share in His holiness:

> For it was fitting that he, for whom and by whom all things exist, in bringing many sons to glory, should make the founder of their salvation perfect through suffering. For he who sanctifies and those who are sanctified all have one source. That is why he is not ashamed to call them brothers. —Hebrews 2:10-11

Do you want true and everlasting joy in your life? Then you must be holy. Sin will not provide us any amount of true joy and happiness. Sin masquerades itself as permanently fulfilling only to pull the old bait 'n switch, deceptively draining us of all true joy. Happiness does not necessitate holiness. Holiness necessitates happiness. So what do we do?

## THE DISCIPLINE OF ABIDING

In John 15:1-11, Jesus says to His disciples:

> I am the true vine, and my Father is the vinedresser. Every branch in me that does not bear fruit he takes away, and every branch that does bear fruit he prunes, that it may bear more fruit. Already you are clean because of the word that I have spoken to you. Abide in me, and I in you. As the branch cannot bear fruit by itself, unless it abides in the vine, neither can you, unless you abide in me. I am the vine; you are the branches. Whoever abides in me and I in him, he it is that bears much fruit, for apart from me you can do nothing. If anyone does not abide in me he is thrown away like a branch and withers; and the branches are gathered, thrown into the fire, and burned. If you abide in me, and my words abide in you, ask whatever you wish, and it will be done for you. By this my Father is glorified, that you bear much fruit and so prove to be my disciples. As the Father has loved me, so have I loved you. Abide in my love. If you keep my commandments, you will abide in my love, just as I have kept my Father's commandments and abide in his

> love. These things I have spoken to you, that my joy may be in you, and that your joy may be full.

Notice that the goal of Jesus' teaching is the fullness of joy in the believer. This is simultaneously linked to giving glory to the Father (the vinedresser). As John Piper often quips, "God is most glorified in us when we are most satisfied in Him."[41] God's glory is maximized in the life of a believer when God's glory is enjoyed. But I don't want to get too far ahead of myself.

In this passage, Jesus is explaining Himself and His relationship as the True Israelite (vine) to His disciples. If joy is to be obtained, then obedience must be cultivated. If obedience is to be cultivated, then Jesus says, "Abide in my love." Abiding is a permanent fixation and steadfast resolve to be connected to Jesus. The word denotes the idea of a dwelling place. To abide with Jesus is to encamp in Him. Apart from Christ we can do nothing (vs. 5). A branch does not bear fruit apart from its life source. Nourishment happens when the believer abides, dwells, or encamps in Christ. Jesus later reminds them that they didn't choose Him, but He chose them, "And appointed [them] that [they] should go and bear fruit and that [their] fruit should abide" (vs. 16). The question then becomes, how do we abide?

To start, abiding means committing. "I have sworn an oath and confirmed it, to keep your righteous rules" (Ps. 119:106). Jerry Bridges warns,

> When we commit ourselves to the pursuit of holiness, we need to ensure that our commitment is actually to God, not simply to a holy lifestyle or a set of moral values.[42]

This danger cannot be overstated. We cannot commit to holiness and expect to win. It's not enough. The believer must commit himself to God, first, and then the path to sanctification

---

[41] John Piper, *The Dangerous Duty of Delight* (Colorado Springs, CO: Multnomah Books, 2011), 15.

[42] Jerry Bridges, *The Discipline of Grace* (Colorado Springs, CO: NavPress, 2006), 148.

can begin. Our commitment to walking this path of godliness is a commitment to walk *towards God.* This is partly what Jesus is getting at in the passage at hand. Abiding requires a commitment to ascertain the goal, namely, God. Believers who wish to be holy are believers who wish to get God. Holy people long to abide in God and *then* receive the fullness of joy.

Abiding also requires that we clarify whose joy we are after. The fullness of joy that Jesus promises is *His joy*. It's not some separate thing. It can't be. Jesus says that abiding in Him results in the believer *getting His very own joy*. This joy is found in Jesus' obedience to the Father. "I have set the LORD always before me; because he is at my right hand, I shall not be shaken. Therefore my heart is glad, and my whole being rejoices; my flesh also dwells secure" (Ps. 16:8-9). The reason it is possible for us to have joy in this life and in the next is because Jesus perfectly submitted Himself to the Law of God, gaining this favor before the Father on our behalf, and crediting that righteousness to our account. In other words, Jesus abided in the Father, and His "whole being rejoices." That is how we get it—Jesus did it for us.

The reality is, sin can destroy joy. Any shred of disobedience, unbelief, or rejection of the gospel can erode joy in our life. This is partly why David cried out, "Restore to me the joy of your salvation" (Ps. 51:12). Salvation wasn't lost, but joy was. Sin severs this abiding and the immediate result is a loss of joy. As believers if we wish to have happiness, we must first be holy. If we wish to be holy, we must abide. If we wish to abide, we must fight against sin. It's a trap, snare and joy-robber.

A discussion about abiding would be futile without at least a couple of important things to consider. I want to take a moment and talk about prayer, suffering, and the Word of God.

## 1. Prayer

"If we do not abide in prayer, we shall abide in cursed temptations."[43] The reality is, prayer is God's means to protect His children. This is why, when teaching His disciples, Jesus

---

[43] John Owen, *The Works of John Owen*. Ed. William H. Goold. Vol. 6. (Edinburgh: T&T Clark), 126.

says, "Lead us not into temptation" (Lk. 11:4). Prayer is how we abide in Christ. If prayer isn't a focus, then abiding simply won't happen. I often tell my congregation that the number one reason many do not pray is because they do not think they are needy. Prayer is our acknowledgement that we are helpless. How are we to fight against sin? "[Pray] at all times in the Spirit, with all prayer and supplication. To that end keep alert with all perseverance" (Eph. 6:18). The Father longs to hear our prayers, not because He needs new information, but because He uses it for transformation. The person who desires to be holy is a person who knows he is helplessly depraved, unable to change his condition apart from the work of God in his life. It's very simple: either we pray, and God uses that as a means to keep you from stumbling, or we don't pray, and we fall into temptation. Do you want the fullness of joy in you? Abide through prayer.

## 2. Suffering

Jesus said that His followers would suffer persecution in this world, and because of it they would be considered blessed (Matt. 5:11-12). In a day and age where suffering is seen as a major problem for God (perpetuated by those who don't know Him), the believer who wishes to abide in Christ must have a framework for dealing with this issue. While I do not have the space to elaborate, because let's face it, volumes would be required, I do want to make a couple of observations from 2 Corinthians:

> But we have this treasure in jars of clay, to show that the surpassing power belongs to God and not to us. We are afflicted in every way, but not crushed; perplexed, but not driven to despair; persecuted, but not forsaken; struck down, but not destroyed; always carrying in the body the death of Jesus, so that the life of Jesus may also be manifested in our bodies. For we who live are always being given over to death for Jesus' sake, so that the life of Jesus also may be manifested in our mortal flesh. So death is at work in us, but life in you. (2 Cor. 4:7-12)

The apostle Paul is demonstrating the work of his ministry and how the gospel treasure is hidden inside of these "jars of clay" (i.e., our weak human natures), because God gets the glory, not him. Paul's ministry was marked by various trials, sufferings and circumstances, but through it all he has survived for God's glory. All of these sufferings are connected to the old man, the old sinful nature, and Paul makes plain that he is dead to sin and alive to Christ (cf. Rom. 6:11). Paul cannot accomplish anything apart from the grace of God, and because of it, his ministry mirrors the ministry of Jesus as he fills up with the afflictions of Christ (Col. 1:24). He goes on,

> So we do not lose heart. Though our outer self is wasting away, our inner self is being renewed day by day. For this light momentary affliction is preparing for us an eternal weight of glory beyond all comparison, as we look not to the things that are seen but to the things that are unseen. For the things that are seen are transient, but the things that are unseen are eternal. —2 Corinthians 4:16-18

Because we live on this side of the resurrection, these words describe us, too. Paul is not talking about our physical bodies breaking down, but instead our old spiritually dead natures wasting away, paving the way for the new and renewed resurrection-powered natures to come. This is sanctification. The newfound reality of resurrection life in the new creation gives us a new perspective. How can you endure suffering? By seeing it for what it is—light, momentary, and only an affliction to the old, sinful nature. That's what suffering is. And not only this, there is an eternal "weight of glory" that far surpasses anything the mind can imagine as we look to those heavenly things, instead of the sin-plagued earthly things. This is gospel power in suffering. Do you want joy in your life in the midst of suffering? Feel the weight of glory. We can be sorrowful, yet always rejoicing. The sorrow part is easy—just take a quick look at Ecclesiastes. The joy part is hard. Unless you have a larger story of triumph (i.e., the gospel), you can't have joy in suffering, because everything is vanity. Either Jesus wins, or death wins—but not both. What's the source of your joy? Jesus. So abide in Him during your suffering. The resurrection awaits us.

## 3. Scripture

People who want to abide in Christ for the fulness of joy are people who want to be holy. People who want to be holy are people who know they are famished of God's Word. It's not enough to know you're hungry—you must eat. Rugged individualism will not work for you. In the pursuit of holiness, there is no room for self-confidence. We must be God-confident. And how are we God-confident? Through His holy, inerrant, inspired, and perspicuous Word.

The path of sanctification is lined with God's Word. It's not enough to presume God's Word, we must digest His Word. How do we digest it? By storing it up, "I have stored up your word in my heart, that I might not sin against you" (Ps. 119:11).

Christians store up God's Word not because knowledge about it is the end-game, but because we want to be holy. Christians are readers, but not just readers, indulgers. The irony, however, is that we are never full. The more we read and pour over God's Word, the more we want more of it. We are not content with just a bite here and there, but desire to feast on it as much as possible. How else can you abide in Christ? Abide in His Word.

Holy people not only believe in *sola scriptura*, they believe in *tota scriptura*. Not only is the Holy Word our sole authority, but *all* of it is our authority. Believers who are looking to be holy are believers who are looking to all of God's Word for the renewal of their minds (Rom. 12:2). We cry out with the Psalmist, "My soul clings to the dust; give me life according to your word!" (Ps. 119:25). Life without God's Word is dust, so we beg of God through the power of His sufficient Word to quench our unending thirst (Ps. 42:1-2; cf. 2 Tim. 3:16-17). We also heed the words of the apostle Paul to "let the word of Christ dwell in [us] richly" (Col. 3:16). Like our precious Savior, Jesus, we memorize Scripture, pour over Scripture and hunger for righteousness found in Scripture so as to defeat the enemy (Matt. 4:1-11). Do you wish to abide in Christ and experience the fullness of joy found only in Him? Then store up God's Word in your heart every single day.

Jared Wilson explains the dynamic of joy:

> Joy is an implication of the gospel, but is not implied for the Christian life—it is commanded. It is not optional . . . Joy is deeper than happiness, but like happiness, joy is always circumstantial. Because the gospel is true, then, even when we aren't happy we can know the deeper joy because the circumstances of God's goodness and love. On the permanent condition of God's unrelenting grace, joy is a permanent possibility . . . Indeed, not to rejoice is sin.[44]

The discipline of abiding requires this perspective outlined by Wilson. Joy is an implication, though not implied—commanded. We do not get to decide if we want to be joyful or not, we must rejoice. Not rejoicing in God is sin because He is infinitely worthy of our adoration, and to *not* give Him glory that is due His name is treason. This is crucial for the discipline of abiding. Our abiding is our work, Jesus doesn't do our part for us. But the unending joy we receive from doing so is breathtaking. The gospel gives us the power, through prayer, suffering, and the Word of God to endure, abide, grow, and be holy. In order to receive this joy, we must be sorry for our sin, but not because we got caught, because we hurt God. We must fight to believe that we are no longer under sin's dominion and because of it, there's always a way out (1 Cor. 10:13). We must no longer blame shift, but instead own our shortcomings. Abiding requires honesty, patience, obedience, and other fruit of the Spirit. Do you wish to abide?

---

[44] Jared C. Wilson, *Gospel Deeps* (Wheaton, IL: Crossway, 2012), 82-84.

## CONCLUDING THOUGHTS

Those who wish to be holy *will* themselves to praise. You can't praise what you don't prize.[45] You can't prize what you don't understand. This has been the aim of this book. To lay out the path of sanctification by defining terms, giving tools, and challenging you to endure. Oftentimes the pursuit of holiness is packaged as a process, or journey whereby one will eventually "arrive." This is only true when we reach glorification. But what about the here and now? Sanctification is worked out each and every day as we take up our cross and follow Jesus, living as missionaries and sojourns for Him. Sanctification is about becoming what you have already been declared to be by grace. It's not about becoming a better you. It's about the Spirit conforming you to the image of Christ.

You see, followers of Jesus who have no theological framework for repentance and faith, baptism, communion, church discipline, missional praxis for making disciples, or commitment to the local church aren't following the Jesus of Scripture. They are following the Jesus of their imagination. The fight to be holy requires doctrinal precision, patience, honesty and unrelenting faithfulness. The gospel is not obscure! If the path of sanctification is ever going to work we must rely on the all-consuming, God-glorying, Christ-honoring gospel of Jesus Christ. And perhaps then we can pray alongside the apostle Paul:

> Now may our God and Father himself, and our Lord Jesus, direct our way to you, and may the Lord make you increase and abound in love for one another and for all, as we do for you, so that he may establish your hearts blameless in holiness before our God and Father, at the coming of our Lord Jesus with all his saints. —1 Thessalonians 3:11-13
>
> Now may the God of peace himself sanctify you completely, and may your whole spirit and soul and body be kept blameless at the coming of our Lord Jesus Christ. He who

---

[45] I may have heard or read Dr. John Piper say this somewhere. Consider this my attribution to him.

calls you is faithful; he will surely do it. —1 Thessalonians 5:23-24)

# ABOUT THE AUTHOR

**Jason M. Garwood** (M.Div., Th.D.) is lead pastor of Colwood Church in Caro, Michigan. He and his wife Mary have three children. You can connect with him online via twitter: @jasongarwood. He also blogs at www.JasonGarwood.com.

MORE RESOURCES FROM G4S BOOKS AT
**GRACEFORSINNERS.COM**

MATHEW B. SIMS

In Scripture, parents are instructed to teach their kids how to love God and are commanded to saturate their home with the gospel (Deut 4:9, 6:1-7; Eph 6:10). Husbands and wives are commanded to mirror Jesus in their marriages (Eph 5:22-33). We understand these commands in light of the gospel—in light of Jesus Christ (2 Cor 4:6). Jesus is the hero of our families.

That's what *A Household Gospel* is about. It's ordinary means rooted in an extraordinary gospel. It's about starting the great commission in our homes. It's about rehearsing the gospel story when we sit to eat, lay down to sleep, rise up in the morning, and everywhere in between.

www.ingramcontent.com/pod-product-compliance
Lightning Source LLC
LaVergne TN
LVHW041232080426
835508LV00011B/1169

* 9 7 8 0 6 9 2 3 5 0 2 8 7 *